LOUDOUN DISCOVERED

Communities, Corners & Crossroads

LOUDOUN DISCOVERED

Communities, Corners
&
Crossroads

Volume Three
The Hunt Country & Middleburg

Eugene M. Scheel

Presented by
The Friends of the Thomas Balch Library
Leesburg, Virginia

This book was manufactured in the United States of America.
Library of Congress Cataloging-in-Publication Data

Scheel, Eugene
Loudoun discovered: communities, corners, and crossroads /
vol. 3 Middleburg and the hunt country
Bibliography: p.
Includes index.
ISBN 0-0724754-2-7 (pbk.)

Cover design by Suzanne Stanton Chadwick
Chadwick Design Incorporated

Cover art from a mural painting by William Woodward

Book design by Janet MacDonald Manthos

Contents

List of Maps

Foreword

The Revolutionary War, the Civil War, the Civil Rights Movement, and many of our nation's other major events have directly impacted Loudoun County. Its history, however, has been shaped largely by the individuals and groups of people who settled and developed the county. *Loudoun Discovered* is a collection of the stories of this early settlement and development and of the gradual transition of crossroads and communities into villages and towns.

In 1975, Eugene Scheel, asked Jim Birchfield, editor of the *Loudoun Times-Mirror* if he could write a series of articles on the history of every town, village, and crossroads hamlet in Loudoun. They would be published to coincide with the U. S. Bicentennial. From his large collection of oral histories and extensive research into court records, church documents, and old maps, Gene developed very rich material, and he produced some 120 articles.

Gene's articles explained why particular settlements began and how they grew or languished. The stories brought out, among other things, how the establishment of trunpike roads and post offices affected development hundreds of years ago. In the 19th-century railroads played this role. During the past 50-or-so-years, it has been modern highways, waater and sewer lines, and airports.

The first broad documentation of the contribution of African Americans to the heritage of Loudoun County was presented in Gene's articles. His stories of the very small African American communities, such as St. Louis, Conklin, and Stewartown, brought them new and deserved recognition.

Late last year, Marty Hiatt, a respected genealogist and a good friend of the Thomas Balch Library, suggested to me that the Friends of the Library publish Gene's articles in book form. For more than 10 years, Marty had wanted to do this on her own. Her thought had been to use the book to raise funds for the Library. Marty had, in fact, taken the first steps on the project: she had scanned all of the articles and converted them into electronic form for editing.

I found strong support for taking on this project from fellow members of the Friends' Board. In addition, the Board members came up with some excellent suggestions for the books–adding maps and a comprehensive index, for example.And the stories would be organized by regions of the county so they could be published in five volumes that would be relatively inexpensive and thus appeal to a broad audience.

The team assembled to prepare the articles for publication consisted of Gene Scheel, Marty Hiatt, Margaret Clarridge and Janet Manthos. Gene's assignment was to update and edit all of the articles and prepare the maps, some 25 among the five volumes. Marty provided guidance and counsel. Margaret checked spelling, punctuation, and consistancy, and Janet handled the desktop publishing, located photographs, prepared the index, and dealt with the printer. The Friends very much appreciate the efforts of these four individuals. They have certainly worked as a team.

The Friends give a special thank you to Arthur Arundel, publisher of the *Loudoun Times-Mirror,* for approving the request to publish Gene Scheel's articles.

If you know Gene or meet him at some point, you will agree, I am sure, that *Loudoun Discovered* is delivered in his uniquely informal and casual voice. In fact, as you read these stories you can easily picture Gene sitting by the wood stove in his Waterford office, gathering these tales and exchanging interpretations with local raconteurs. Gene has reminded us that memories, especially those of our wonderful senior citizens, are not always accurate; as we know, different folk will recall the same event differently. This is not a reason, however, for excluding these recollections from a publication such as this. They help amplify the facts and bring these facts to life.

We hope reading these volumes will stimulate you to do some further digging into the history of this beautiful and historic county. The very best place to do that, bar none, is the Thomas Balch Library in Leesburg. It is a great place to carry out your research.

Enjoy!

Fred Morefield, President
The Friends of the Thomas Balch Library Inc.

Leesburg, Virginia
October 2002

Introduction

An old-timer might have referred to this stretch from Aldie west to the Blue Ridge as lower Loudoun. Today it's broadly "Middleburg," for, indeed, the town's zip code, 20186, takes in the greater part of the area included in this third volume of *Loudoun Discovered.* Sometimes I call the region "along the Ashby's Gap Turnpike," a name for Route 50 discarded a decade ago when both Loudoun and Fauquier, the two counties bisected by the road, opted for John Mosby Highway, to honor the Confederate partisan ranger who roamed about its parts for fewer than three years.

One encounters Ranger Mosby throughout this area, in fact and in legend, and at the eastern gateway to the old pike there's a sign designating the John Singleton Mosby Heritage Area. Its domain takes in the entire road corridor, as well as much of western Loudoun to the north—plus vast regions of Clarke, Fauquier, Prince William, and Warren Counties.

But it's not only for Colonel Mosby that the area is named. To quote the squib on the map designating the area in 1995, the creation of a heritage area "increase[s] knowledge and appreciation of the rich historic and natural qualities which distinguish the region. Bordered by natural features and historic travelways, the Mosby Heritage Area retains much of the landscape and landmarks of the past three centuries."

The quote is an apt one, for along many of the area's dirt roads and in many of its villages, it is not hard to be transported into a bygone realm. Vestiges of the 17th century, when the peaceful Sioux Indians hunted big game here, survive only in the guise of archeological sites. About 1670 the war like Susquehanna drove the Sioux from the area. Yes, they are the forebears of the Indians who brought you Custer's Last Stand in 1876.

I also mention the Piscataway, featured in volume two, who before moving to Potomac River islands where they could find more fish, their favorite meal, lived in a large village south of Middleburg. That the population of local river denizens was scant in this area during the 1690s is evident in the stream name "Hunger Run."

The European settlement pattern here is the same as that of the east and middle of Loudoun: Tidewater speculators of the late 1720s through the 1760s amassing large tract to which they sent their slaves and an overseer or two. Again, they mainly planted corn, wheat, small grains, and some tobacco.

Surveyors plotting the speculators' tracts didn't know much about soil types, but they knew that where oak, poplar, and walnut grew together, the soil was prime. These were the lands they sought for their clients. As decades passed, adjoining landowners found that many boundaries of these early surveys overlapped, and scores of land suits and court cases help to fill barrister's pockets through the early 19th century.

Several of these early surveys hark back to American Indian times, in that they mention "Poisoned fields." The surveyors reckoned that the water was "poisoned" under these sometimes vast areas of poison ivy, creeper, and briar bushes, but in reality they were tracts the Indians had once burned. The burnings had taken place to induce grassland, where the deer and buffalo roamed—the big-game staples of the Sioux.

U. S. forester Hu Maxwell, writing some decades ago, commented that if the white men had not come to America when they did, the Indians would have burned the whole continent down. Government employees today would be wary of putting such words into print.

Along the Ashby's Gap Turnpike corridor these white men—and their slaves—tilled the best soils in Loudoun, and by the early 1800s this westward extension of lower Loudoun had become the place to live and the place to buy. Raw land prices best $20 and $30 an acre in a time when the average daily wage was about a dollar.

And to bring the produce of that land to market there was the turnpike, complete in 1819. Along its length the main villages and towns would spring up—the genesis of the first unknown entrepreneur, who decades before, decided to fill his wagon with manufactured staples and bring them up-country where he could sell them at a profit at the first area "store." Area kingpin Leven Powell, speaking of the 1780s, remarked that in the country there "were little stores everywhere." These "storehouses" as they were called, generally arose at places where people passed and congregated. These crossroads and mills then evolved into the villages featured in this and other volumes of *Loudoun Discovered.*

Colonel Powell, Revolutionary hero and friend of George Washington, was the first of many luminaries on the political scene who would first live by the turnpike. From Independence to the Civil War, nine area politicians represented Loudoun in the U. S. Senate and Congress, and in the state legislature and state constitutional conventions. After the war—zero—the politicians took to riding horses.

The war—and in old Virginia there's only one war—put the landscape to ruin, partly because of troops, mostly Union, foraging for food and livestock as they hunted for Mosby, the elusive partisan ranger. Then there were the June 17-21, 1863, cavalry battles along the pike from Aldie to Upperville—a prelude to Gettysburg. And then came the "burning raid" of Union forces from the Shenandoah Valley, November 28-29, 1864; they destroyed crops, barns, and mills, reasoning that Mosby would commandeer them for Confederate uses. But prime soils dictated a quick recovery, and the area regained its agricultural pre-eminence within a decade after the war's end in 1865.

It was not too long afterwards that Northern money began to invest in the region's real estate, partly because of long-established family liaisons. But mainly, the shrewd expender of funds saw in the turnpike corridor a region reminiscent of the hills of New York and New England, but with soils that far surpassed Northern dirt. And it was no surprise that many of these investors spent leisure hours riding to the hounds, a favorite sport among landed Northern gentry.

Foxhunting had also been a fixture in the Virginia Piedmont, even back in the 18th century, when Thomas, sixth Lord Fairfax rode with his contemporaries. And thus in the Piedmont, North and South had common ground, both in the sport and the raising of the steeds necessary to the chase.

In 1905 much of the sporting world attuned itself to newspaper accounts of a 12-meet foxhunting duel between an English pack of hounds and an American pack. In a land described as "Piedmont Valley, Virginia," in reality the country about Middleburg and Upperville, the riders set out that October and November.

Of the area a *Boston Transcript* reporter wrote words presaging those of the Mosby Heritage people nearly a century later:

> …the Blue Ridge heaves up its rounded breast, mottled with woodland and cultivated fields. As far to the east, the Bull Run Mountains wall the valley…Today the foxhunters

gallop where a generation ago Stonewall Jackson rode, master of a sterner game. This valley is redolent of wartime memories. ...a rolling country, free from stone and checkered fields of winter wheat, now in its tenderest hues, corn fields stacked with heavy harvest, and grass taking on the sober garb of late autumn.

This meet popularized the area, where now, the widows of Confederate officers, or their heirs, were beginning to part with their former plantations. It was a marriage of Blue and Gray, and the former were rich. Listen to this *Fortune* article of 1930:

"Smart Middleburg:...Once a dusty, drowsing Piedmont village, the foxhunters have now taken it over lock, stock, and barrel (lots of barrels)...Middleburg is the Valhalla of the young married Valkyries, who drink, dance and overbid from dinner table to next morning's meet. Here fledgling millionaires are completely exonerated from all affections about work."

But in the main, this is not the Middleburg, Upperville, and Ashby's Gap Turnpike country featured in this book. Rather, we present the story of average people, whose stores and shops service the foxhunters, and whose skills as maids, gardeners, and farmers make life pleasant. I'm reminded of words spoken to me by Middleburg councilman Jack Turner: "Remember, most of us have never been on a horse."

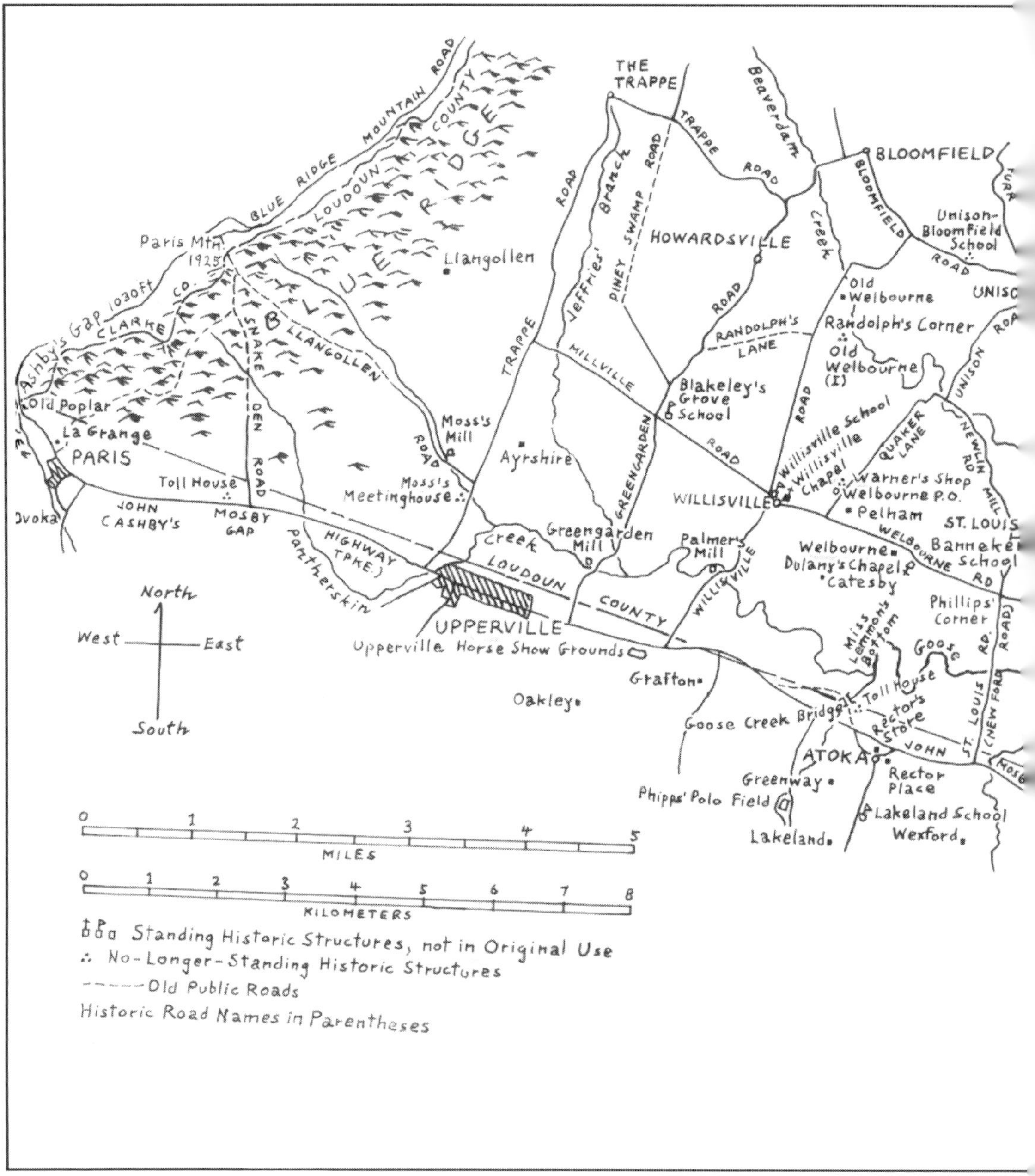

THE TRAPPE
BLUE RIDGE MOUNTAIN ROAD
LOUDOUN COUNTY
BLUE RIDGE
Paris Mtn. 1925
Ashby's Gap 1030 ft
CLARKE CO.
Llangollen
LLANGOLLEN
SNAKE DEN ROAD
Old Poplar
La Grange
PARIS
Toll House
JOHN CASHBY'S
MOSBY GAP
HIGHWAY TPKE.)
Panther Skin
Moss's Mill
ROAD
Moss's Meetinghouse
TRAPPE ROAD
Jeffries' Branch
DINEY SWAMP ROAD
TRAPPE ROAD
Beaverdam Creek
HOWARDSVILLE
ROAD
RANDOLPH'S LANE
MILLVILLE ROAD
Ayrshire
Blakeley's Grove School
GREENGARDEN
Greengarden Mill
Creek
LOUDOUN COUNTY
UPPERVILLE
Upperville Horse Show Grounds
Palmer's Mill
WILLISVILLE
BLOOMFIELD
BLOOMFIELD ROAD
Unison-Bloomfield School
Old Welbourne
Randolph's Corner
Old Welbourne (I)
ROAD
UNISON ROAD
Willisville School
Willisville Chapel
WILLISVILLE
QUAKER LANE
NEWLIN MILL RD
Warner's Shop
Welbourne P.O.
Pelham
ST. LOUIS
Banneker School
Welbourne
Dulany's Chapel
Catesby
WELBOURNE RD
Phillips' Corner
Miss Lemmon's Bottom
Goose
ST. LOUIS RD. (NEW FORD ROAD)
Toll House
Rector's Store
JOHN
Grafton
Oakley
Goose Creek Bridge
ATOKA
Greenway
Rector Place
Phipps' Polo Field
Lakeland School
Lakeland
Wexford
North
West
East
South
0 1 2 3 4 5
MILES
0 1 2 3 4 5 6 7 8
KILOMETERS
Standing Historic Structures, not in Original Use
No-Longer-Standing Historic Structures
Old Public Roads
Historic Road Names in Parentheses

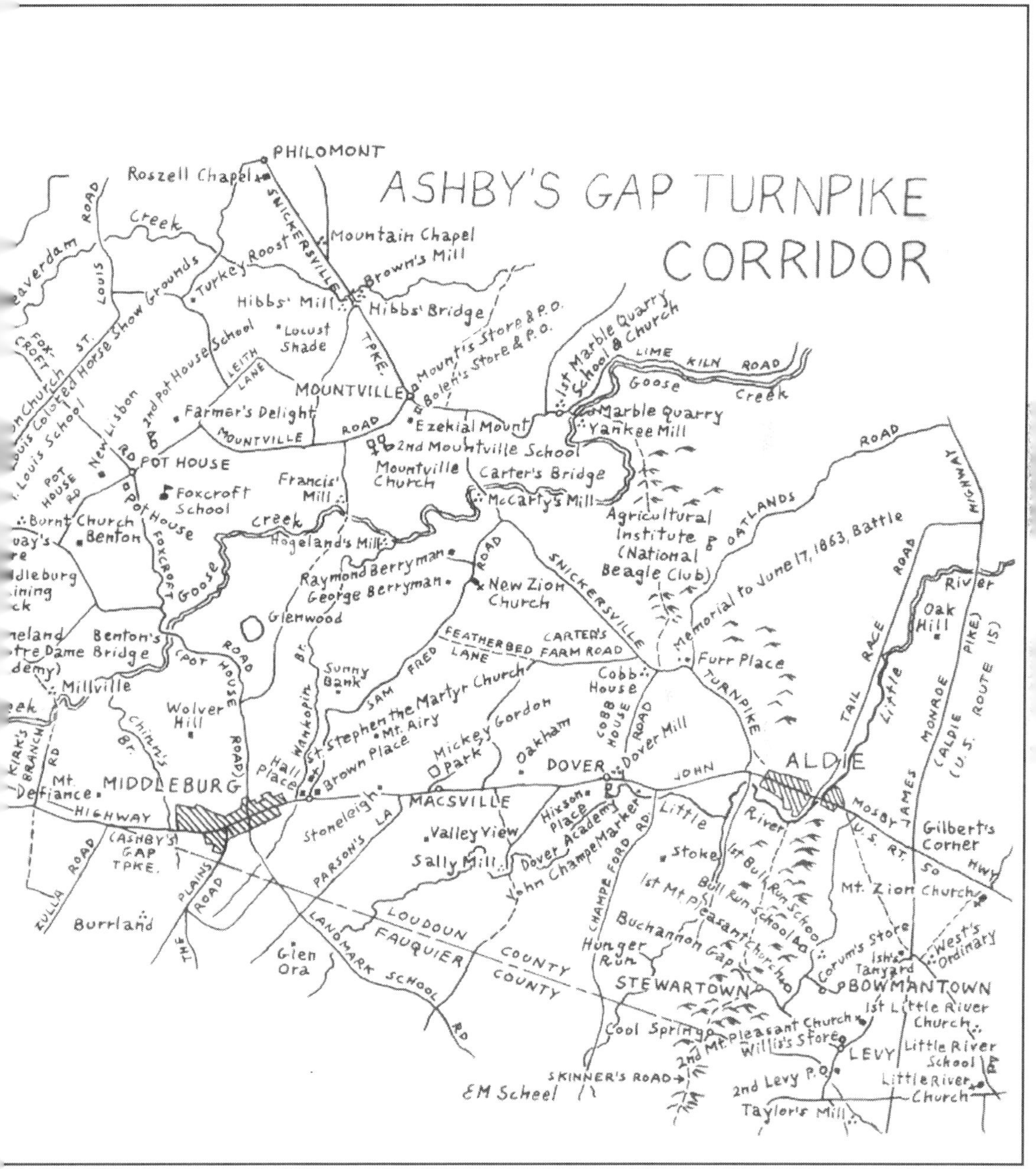
ASHBY'S GAP TURNPIKE CORRIDOR
PHILOMONT
Roszell Chapel
Mountain Chapel
Brown's Mill
Hibbs' Mill
Hibbs' Bridge
Turkey Roost
Locust Shade
Beaverdam Creek
ST. LOUIS ROAD
SNICKERSVILLE TPKE.
Colored Horse Show Grounds
2nd Pot House School
LEITH LANE
MOUNTVILLE
Mount's Store & P.O.
Bolen's Store & P.O.
1st Marble Quarry School & Church
LIME KILN ROAD
Goose Creek
Marble Quarry
Yankee Mill
Farmer's Delight
MOUNTVILLE ROAD
Ezekial Mount
2nd Mountville School
Mountville Church
Carter's Bridge
McCarty's Mill
Francis' Mill
New Lisbon
POT HOUSE
POT HOUSE RD
Foxcroft School
Pot House
FOXCROFT
Burnt Church
Benton
Goose Creek
Hogeland's Mill
Agricultural Institute (National Beagle Club)
OATLANDS ROAD
HIGHWAY
Raymond Berryman
George Berryman
New Zion Church
ROAD
SNICKERSVILLE TURNPIKE
Memorial to June 17, 1863, Battle
Glenwood
Benton's Bridge
Notre Dame Academy
Millville
POT HOUSE ROAD
FEATHERBED LANE
CARTER'S FARM ROAD
SAM FRED
Sunny Bank
Wolver Hill
Chinn's Br.
Wankopin Br.
St. Stephen the Martyr Church
Mt. Airy
Brown Place
Hall Place
Mickey Gordon Park
Oakham
Cobb House
COBB HOUSE ROAD
Furr Place
Dover Mill
DOVER
ALDIE
River
Oak Hill
TAIL RACE
Little
MONROE
JAMES
(ALDIE PIKE) (U.S. ROUTE 15)
KIRK'S BRANCH RD
Mt. Defiance
MIDDLEBURG
HIGHWAY
(ASHBY'S GAP TPKE.)
Stoneleigh
PARSON'S LA
MACSVILLE
Valley View
Sally Mill
Hixson Place
Dover Academy
John Champe Marker
JOHN
Little River
CHAMPE FORD RD.
Stoke
1st Bull Run School
Bull Run School
1st Mt. Pleasant Church
MOSBY U.S. RT. 50 HWY
Gilbert's Corner
Mt. Zion Church
PLAINS ROAD
THE
ZULLA ROAD
Burrland
LOUDOUN COUNTY
FAUQUIER COUNTY
LANDMARK SCHOOL RD
Glen Ora
Hunger Run
Buchannon Gap
STEWARTOWN
Corum's Store
Ish's Tanyard
West's Ordinary
BOWMANTOWN
1st Little River Church
Cool Spring
2nd Mt. Pleasant Church
Willis's Store
LEVY
Little River School
SKINNER'S ROAD
2nd Levy P.O.
Little River Church
Taylor's Mill
EM Scheel

Middleburg

Halfway Stop Between Winchester And Alexandria

In 1731, Colonel Robert Carter's 68th and last year, he as land agent for Thomas, sixth Lord Fairfax, advised fellow Lancaster County planters Charles Burgess, William Stamps, and Rawleigh Chinn to invest in Piedmont land, of which the colonel already owned some 40,000 acres, 21,000 in future Loudoun. And that early summer, surveyor Thomas Barber hacked his way into the backwoods and determined the bounds and notched the metes of a 3,300-acre tract for Rawleigh Chinn. Fifty-six year later his grandsons and granddaughters would see a fragment of this land–perhaps with some animosity–become Middleburg.

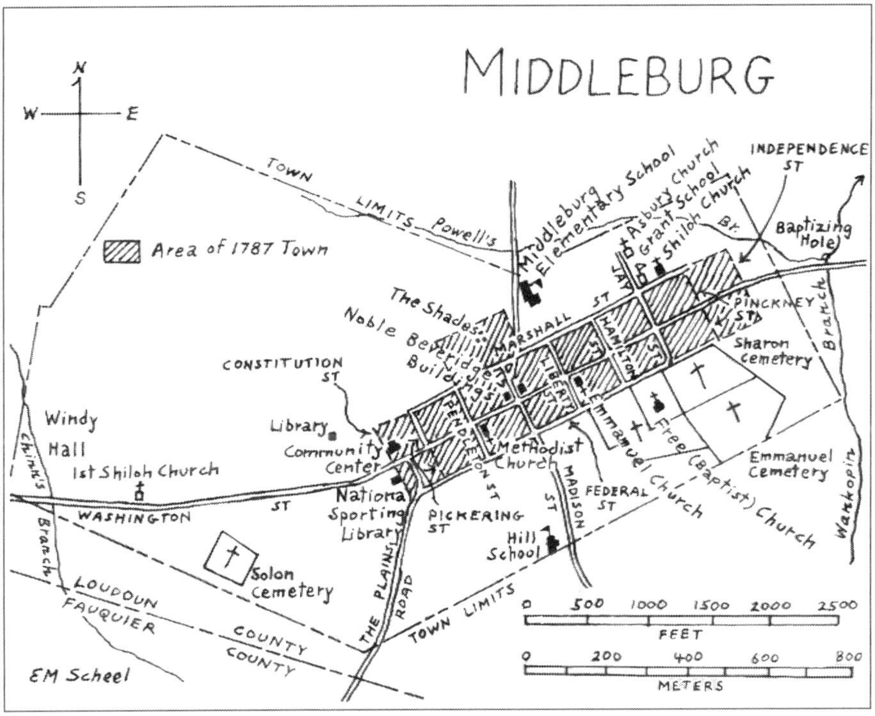

The deed to Rawleigh Chinn was recorded in Northern Neck land books at Robert Carter's office at Corotoman on December 7, 1731. For his 3,300 acres Chinn paid a yearly rental of sixty-six shillings–"one Shilling Sterling" for each fifty acres. As with most land rentals in

Lord Fairfax's vast domain, the rent was due September 29, Michaelmas, the Feast of St. Michael the Archangel, one of four English quarter days when rents and debts were due. Lord Fairfax reserved "Royal Mines and a full third Part of all Lead, Copper, Tin, Coals, Iron Mines and Iron Ore," another standard leasing provision.

Thomas Barber's survey is measured by perches (16 ½ feet), "beginning at a Marked Red Oak in and a Locust Field and Corner to a Tract of Land belonging to Mr. Charlesses Burges of Lancaster Country." The distinctive oak was often a survey corner, but as we shall see, one had to be careful if one named the species of oak. The only other identifiable points were "a Red Oak on a point near Goose Creek," a hickory in a corner to William Stamps' line, and "a Chestnut Oak on a High Point and Corner to the said Stamps' and Mr. Burges, thence along the said Burges his Line." On the reverse side of the crude map accompanying the survey, Barber names his client "W. Rawleigh Chin." Rawleigh did not use his first name–Walter.

His grandfather, the Reverend Thomas Chynn, had sailed to Virginia with Sir Walter Raleigh, but a century later Rawleigh Chinn had strayed from his roots. He repeatedly beat his wife, the former Esther Ball. (Her sister Mary had married Augustine Washington, father of George.) The court granted Mrs. Chinn a separation allowance—as she had five children—and Rawleigh Chinn continued his errant ways via a long affair with Esther's widowed sister, Margaret Ball Downman. Margaret bore Rawleigh Chinn three more children.

Of Mr. Chinn's eight children, seven were boys, and each received land by terms of Rawleigh Chinn's 1741 will. The three children of Margaret Downman were to each receive 500 acres of the 1731 grant only if they had children. All did. In total, six of Rawleigh Chinn's sons inherited segments of the original grant, but only two, Elijah and Charles, both children of Mrs. Downman, settled there by the summer of 1751.

Neither man, however, was the first settler of future Middleburg. That honor belongs to Edward Hughes, who was a Cameron Parrish vestryman and owner of one slave in 1749. In an 1811 court deposition, Thomas Chinn, son of Elijah, recited from family lore that in 1731 surveyor Thomas Barber and his poleman "were shown by one Hughes, a man living on the land who acted as their pilot." Another 1811 court deponent states the name "Hughes's Road" was, in the mid 18th century, the name for present Route 50.

The court case I've alluded to concerned 700 acres in dispute between Rawleigh "Sailor" Chinn II, son of Elijah Chinn, and Colonel Leven Powell, a Revolutionary War hero and area resident since 1757, at least, when Mr. Powell "achieved his Majority"—became 21.

The Chinn-Powell land dispute as to whom owned what had first flared up in 1772, and lasted for a decade before it was amicably settled. Then, on the first day of 1793 the issue arose again, when, court records stated that two of Mr. Powell's lessees,

> Francis Wronghead and Ferdinando Dreadnought," came to "Timothy Trytitle's" tenement, and "with force and Arms to wit with Guns, Staves & Sticks...ejected expelled and amoved the said Timothy."

First, the aforementioned names in court records are known as "legal fictions." If you know your classical literature, Messrs. Wronghead, Dreadnought, and Trytitle were characters in John Bunyan's *Pilgrim's Progress.*

Second, eight years later Powell's tenants, "Francis and Ferdinando" were not prosecuted. But Rawleigh Chinn appealed to the District Superior Court at Haymarket and reversed the lower court's decision in 1803.

And another eight years later, with Leven Powell dead, his eldest son Burr Powell, again sought to eject Rawleigh Chinn's tenants. Besides the significant acreages involved—never before or again would 700 acres be contested as to ownership—the Powell family home, The Shades, stood a few hundred feet from the boundary in question. So did the high point of the acreage claimed by Mr. Chinn, an ideal building site and site of his family graveyard.

Deponents before the court speaking on the Powell's behalf immediately questioned the character of Thomas Chinn, who had kept his grandfather Rawleigh (I)'s record. Nearly a quarter of a century before, Thomas Chinn had assisted Burr Powell's father in establishing the town of Middleburg, but that friendship, apparently, had been overruled in the legal sparring. Leading townsmen, however, quickly spoke up for Mr. Chinn with such comments as "a man of strict veracity" and "integrity stands unimpeached."

So the Powell lawyers then harped on Thomas Barber's surveys by bringing George Love to the witness stand. Mr. Love, by 1811, was considered by many to be the finest surveyor in the Middleburg area and in upper Fauquier. Thirteen years later he would be the first to survey the Loudoun-Fauquier line, which officially moved the town of Upperville from Loudoun into Fauquier. Mr. Love, in answering a loaded question, "have you not discovered that the said Barber was very inaccurate in his plat…?" replied that the long-gone Barber's surveys "were replete with error." The testimony of James N. Fishback brought some levity to this inquisition, which largely questioned happenings of more than a half-century past: Mr. Fishback, notes the case recorder, "recollects hearing Colonel Powell say that he had established a corner there [at Kirk's Branch Road]; that he had jockeyed Chinn out of it, or Chinn had jockeyed him. He does not recollect which."

Twenty-one years after the dispute was entered in the docket, the court reached its decision, April 6, 1814. The Powells had to relinquish all claim to the 700 acres north and east of town, and in exchange the Chinns had to give up the disputed 318 acres north of the pike and east of Kirk's Branch Road that had started the feud in 1772. In the exchange of documents that followed, Powell's deed to Chinn called the solution "a compromise;" Chinn's to Powell called it "an ejectment."

With the families, names would live on. On the high point of the 700 acres the Chinns—probably Samuel Rawleigh Chinn, Rawleigh's son—built their home, Mount Recovery. Samuel would later say he was born on Recovery Hill. Mount Recovery burned during the Civil War—the fire was not related to war events—was rebuilt by 1866, and burned for the final time about the turn of the century. Wolver Hill, built in 1922, stands there today. Not to be outdone, Burr Powell had his Mount Defiance built on the high point of his 318 acres. For many years a Carter tenant house, this home, remodeled and enlarged, stands in Middleburg Downs.

Hughes's Road, more commonly called the Belhaven Road–Belhaven being the pre-1749 name for the seaport of Alexandria–nearly bisected these old Chinn and Powell plantations. And this road, now Middleburg's Washington Street and the county's John Mosby Highway, would determine the future town's location. Leven Powell's home, The Shades, stood but a few hundred yards from the road, and the lane to the home, and another lane leading south–now Madison Street–had become a crossroads of some importance.

Since 1779, when Colonel Powell was elected to Virginia General Assembly, The Shades had welcomed many visitors—to discuss politics and to hear of the Revolution. The colonel had suffered at Valley

Forge during the winter of 1777-78.

At the same time the Belhaven Road's wagon traffic was increasing, and often the produce–laden vehicles, pulled by four- and six-horse teams came from the Shenandoah Valley. They were stopping by the crossroads, possibly at a hostelry later described as operated by John McFarland. The crossroads was just about midway between the Belhaven Road's two main destinations, Alexandria and Winchester. Between the two, the nearest stopovers of any account, were Rust's Ordinary below the east brow of the Blue Ridge and Lacey's Ordinary on the Carolina Road. Both taverns were more than seven miles away.

Winchester and Alexandria were then among the six largest towns in Virginia, and I'm reminded that years ago a Loudouner was considered to have a degree of sophistication if "he had been to Winchester or Alexandria."

PHOTO COURTESY KENNETH GILPIN JR.

The crossroads in 1926 (by Gen. Billy Mitchell)

By 1787 three of Colonel Powell and wife Sarah's children were storekeepers and shipping merchants in Alexandria, in a highly competitive market. To help his sons by giving them an upcountry outlet for their goods, he set up a retail store at the crossroads that spring. Samuel Love, who had previous experience as an area storekeeper, attended to this first known "town" business.

By October Leven Powell was back in Richmond in the General Assembly, and in somewhat unusual circumstances he forwarded his plea for a town. Somehow he had enticed a band of Pennsylvanians to his 500 acres by the crossroads; they may have been Revolutionary War cronies. And in his petition to the assembly he stated the five Pennsylvanians and three locals were "Lottholders," and in

> "their opinion the Situation of the place bids fair to become a respectable Village, that this consideration induced most of them to remove from Pennsylvania and have great assurances that if the same is established as a Town by Law a number others will shortly become adventurers. We therefore pray that your Honors will pass a Law that a certain Number of Acres may be laid off for a Town & your Petitioners as in duty bound with our prayer."

Below these words Powell penned a brief note to his fellow law-makers: "I have no objection to a Law passing agreeable to the prayer of the above petition."

Another strange element of the petition concerned its eight signatures. All were written by the same person, even though the three local petitioners could write, sign their own names, and mark their own "X's."

Nevertheless, on November 2nd 1787, ten days after the petition had arrived, Powell's town was a reality. Fifty of his five hundred acres were to be divided into half-acre lots "with convenient streets." Lot owners were to "have built thereon a dwelling house sixteen feet square, with a brick or stone chimney"—a standard practice.

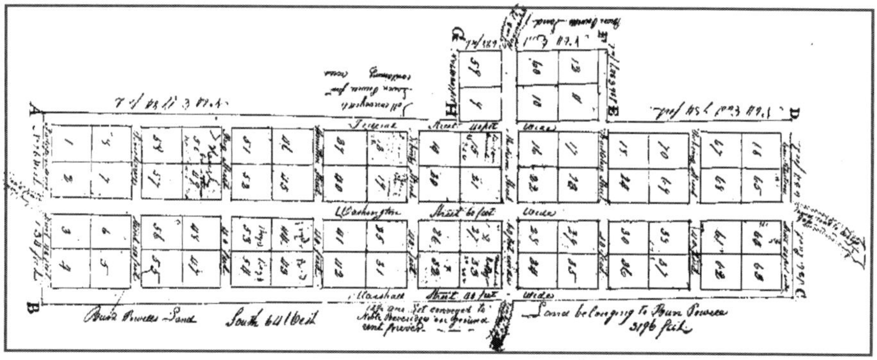

Believed to be Leven Powell's plat, circa 1787-1815

Illustration from the author's collection

From early town deeds we can draw some assumptions. First; Leven Powell was not interested in the money that lots would bring in. He owned more than 1,800 acres of Loudoun land in addition to his massive western-land holdings, 22 slaves twelve and older, 18 horses, 24 head of cattle, a two-wheeled chair, and at least one sloop. The first payments for his lots were not due until January 1, 1800. Second; Colonel Powell wanted his family to have a continuing interest in the town and thus chose to rent his lots in perpetuity rather than sell them. The buildings and land could be sold, but a yearly ground rent would always be due to the Powell family. Through the nineteenth century most property owners paid an annual fee to the family, and not until 1916 did the state declare ground rents void. Ground rents, incidentally, were popular in Maryland, home of Colonel Powell's father, William. Third; in a time of unstable economic conditions, Leven Powell required payment to be made in "current Money" or in pistoles, a gold piece worth three and one-third Spanish Milled Dollars. Fourth; while rental terms were generous, if the required dwelling were not put up within a certain time (usually a year), and if the rent were thirty days delinquent, the property reverted to Colonel Powell or his heirs.

Street names appear on all early Middleburg deeds, and as the original town plat does not survive, one cannot say when Leven Powell chose the names, but they may have taken fruition after he returned as a Loudoun delegate to the June 1788 Richmond Convention that ratified the 1787 Federal Constitution by a vote of 89-79. Powell voted with the majority on each issue; his fellow delegate, Stevens Thomson Mason of Selma, north of Leesburg, voted with the minority.

Independence Street on the east, Constitution Street on the west, Marshall Street on the north, and Federal Street on the south, enclosed the town. Marshall Street was named for Fauquier's John Marshall, who suggested calling the Richmond Convention, and was an elected delegate from his home county. Pinckney Street was named for South Carolinian Charles Pinckney, author of the "Pinckney Draught," a plan from which some thirty provisions were incorporated into the Constitution. Jay Street took its name from New Yorker John Jay, author of five articles in *The Federalist.* Washington and Liberty Streets need no explanation. Madison Street honors Orange County's James Madison, author of twenty-nine essays in *The Federalist.* Hamilton Street was named for New York's Alexander Hamilton, author of fifty-nine essays in *The Federalist* and Virginia's representative to the 1787 Constitutional Convention. Pendleton Street was named for Caroline County's Edmund Pendleton, president of the Richmond Convention, and Pickering Street honors Bay Stater Timothy Pickering, quarter-master general of the Revolutionary armies, and probably a friend of Colonel Powell.

Middleburg also had a post office, established October 2 1797, with Burr Powell the postmaster at a $500 yearly salary (the average wage, a dollar a day). Next April 23, Robert Dagg became deputy postmaster at a $300 salary, and on May 3 postmaster, as Powell, following in his father's stead, began campaigning for a seat in the General Assembly. He won and remained in office through 1807. Dagg held the postmastership until his death in 1815. The post office name was the English "Middleburgh" a spelling that held for nearly a century.

Despite the shady documents authorizing the town, Leven Powell knew a good location when he saw it, and Middleburg prospered. But by the 1820s Aldie, with its huge mill, began to give Middleburg a run for its money. Lest the Burg be surpassed, in 1825 and 1827 townsman Noble Beveridge superintended construction of two near-twin buildings at the Washington and Madison Street corner. Today the 1827 stone structure bears the name Red Fox Inn.

But if you read the sign on the inn it gives the building date as "ca. 1728"—just the fault of an errant sign painter who had dyslexia. But wouldn't you rather eat in a 1728 building than an 1827 one?

PHOTO COURTESY OF SARAH CHAPPELLE

Today's Red Fox Inn, circa 1900

Middleburg incorporated in 1831, meaning that the town now elected nine trustees to run its affairs. The trustees could receive and hold "lands and tenement"; lay out streets, walks, and alleys; organize a fire company; begin a school; "prevent and punish by reasonable fines, the practice of firing guns and running horses"; license shows and public exhibitions; appoint town officers and establish regulations and laws enforced by fines not to exceed $20; place a 75-cent tax on each tithable and on each $100 worth of taxable property; and appoint a town sergeant or tax collector.

Yardley Taylor, the Loudoun Quaker geographer and horticulturist, summarized Middleburg's growth in his glowing descriptions of Loudoun's towns and countryside in Joseph Martin's 1835 *Gazetteer of Virginia.* He counted seventy dwellings and "numerous and inexhaustible wells of the purest and best water." Seven mercantile stores sold an average of $80,000 worth of goods yearly. There were also four physicians, three milliners, two lawyers, two manufacturers of coaches and wagons, two shoemaker's shops (Taylor called them "boot and shoe factories"), two blacksmiths, two tailors, two house carpenters, two saddlers, two mantua makers, a tanner and currier, a chair maker and a cabinet maker. He also noted the Methodist and Free Churches, someone's "classical school," an "English school for males," and two "female academies" and two hotels. In summary "A growing and prosperous village" of 430 persons "surrounded by a beautiful and fertile country. Its situation is elevated and airy—the houses are not crowded,

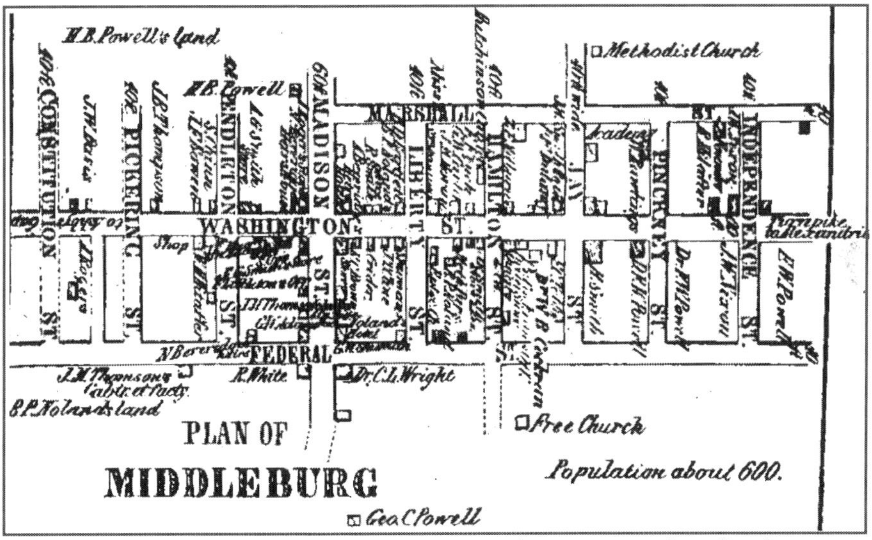

Yardley Taylor's 1853 map of Middleburg

Illustration courtesy Thomas Balch Library

but scattered regularly over several gradually rising eminences."

Samuel Satterthwait, also a Quaker and a town wagon-maker, wrote the one surviving pithy letter describing the town of this era in "9th mo" 1833. It was a very dry season—

> "mills in our neighborhood are stoped from grinding…I don't know what we should do for flour the waggons from over the Blue Ridge Mt. from Frederick & Shenandoah country pass through here on their way to Alexa to Market we stop them to get their flour they are glad to dispose of all they can to lighten their load they generally take form 16 to 12 to 20 Barrel it is considered the best flour that is made & commands a better price. Thee would be astonished to see the quantity of cattle that passes through here in the course of a week for the District & Baltimore markets and sometimes they carry them to Phila…the Black people bring such marketing in town at nights such as potatoes Chickens eggs Apples Peaches Brown Chickens they sell at $1.00 per doz alive…I am confident it is better for a young man in the west."

To mention a few luminaries who come to my mind as builders of the town during the 19th century, I first turn to Richard Cochran, builder of homes and later a physician. Mr. Cochran built or designed nearly every noteworthy town structure during the century's first three decades.

And during the town's three-or-so decades before its 1831 incorporation, it was Burr Powell who managed the civil matters of growth that increased the town's population four-fold.

And in business the persons to cite were the Brouns, Edwin Conway and his wife Catherine. He ran the town's main store and post office from 1839 at age 18, until his death in 1879. Catherine assisted him, often in grief, as the couple lost five children during that period.

Of the post-Civil War era I always think of "Professor" Oliver L. Grant, whose lone mention in the newspapers was as a restaurateur in 1887 serving up "bivalves in all styles." School-board records are not extant to show he was the first principal and long time teacher of the "Middleburg Colored School," as later records call the 1888 building. But that he was a man of note is indicated in the black peoples' name for the institution: Grant School.

And so this essay of the beginnings of a town ends. So many, including me, have covered the Civil War era, and so many have covered the Hunt Country years that began in earnest in the first decade of the last century. For details you can garner hints from this volume's bibliography.

Aldie

When Mill Wheels Turn The Village Hums

As early as 1764, the brothers James and George Mercer, established a small mill at or near the site of the present Aldie Mill. Their father, John Mercer, then owned nearly 4,000 acres on both sides of Bull Run Mountain, including the future village of Aldie. Initially, the village lands were encompassed by a 1,449-acre grant from Thomas, sixth Lord Fairfax to Thomas Owsley in 1740.

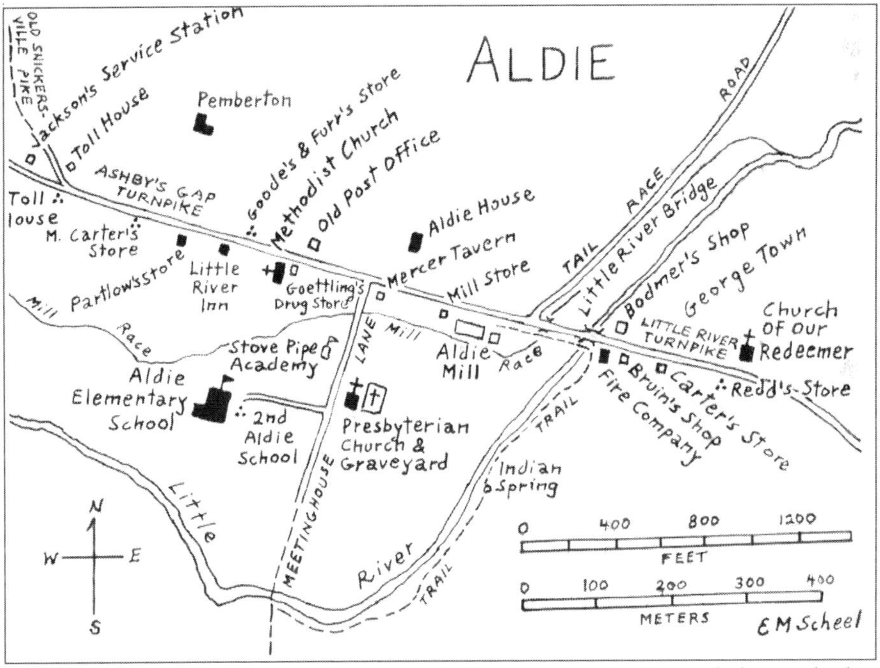

Little River, largest tributary of Goose Creek, flowed through the slight mountain gap, and in the next century the village and its neighborhood would sometimes be called Aldie Gap or just Little River. In the 18th century, Bull Run Mountain was often referred to as the Little River Mountain. Through the gap came the old Belhaven or Ashby's Gap Road, the main road between Alexandria and Winchester, then among the six largest cities in Virginia. Just west of the gap, the Middle or Mountain Road wound northwards toward Williams' or Snickers' Gap. Down this road came wagons laden with grain and produce from the rich Shenandoah and Loudoun Valleys. The meeting place of the Belhaven and Mountain Roads was an ideal one for commerce and manufacturing.

Charles Fenton Mercer, James Mercer's son, settled in Leesburg in 1804, and there practiced law. Late in 1807 he signed an agreement with contractor William Cooke, who was to build a large wheat and corn mill, saw mill, store, miller's house, dwelling house, and combined blacksmith, wheelwright, and cooper (barrel-maker) shop. The deed also mentioned a tavern and wagon shop, but Mr. Cooke did not have to build them. An 1809 survey shows that the mill, store, miller's house, "mansion home," and "spinning house," had been constructed, and the Little River Turnpike from Alexandria had been completed to the mill. The present two-span, stone-arch bridge was not built until 1813.

PHOTO COURTESY THOMAS BALCH LIBRARY

Aldie House, home of Charles F. Mercer

Elected to the General Assembly of Virginia in 1810, Charles Fenton Mercer had his complex of buildings established as a town laid out on 30 acres "at the western extremity of the Little River turnpike road," part of his vast inherited holdings. He named the town Aldie, in honor of his family's ancestral home, Aldie Castle, Perthshire, Scotland. Besides Messrs. Mercer and Cooke, the town's first trustees were Matthew Adam, the Scottish millwright who supervised construction of the millworks; Israel Lacey, keeper of a tavern, two miles southeast of the village; surveyor John Sinclair; farmer James Hixson from Dover, west of the village; William Noland, who had run the close-by sawmill since the fall of 1807; and David Gibson.

An 1811 deed names the 1809 mansion home "Aldie house," and one notes that the Mercer home in Bermuda also bears that name. Mercer did not move to Aldie until 1816, and Emily diZerega, whose family acquired the property in 1842, told why in 1936:

> Charles Fenton Mercer had an unfortunate love affair before he finished the house…even the portico being merely propped up with posts. The bases of the sandstone columns, with which he intended to build an imposing portico, still lie on the side of the adjacent hill…In 1842 he met Augustus diZerega, a wealthy Italian importer from New York, who had some years before come up from Venezuela where his father had settled. Mr. diZerega called on Mr. Mercer at his bank to dispose of some Florida bonds…which had not turned out well. In the course of conversation Mr. Mercer mentioned his 'Aldie' property, which he wished to dispose of. As a result the Florida bonds were exchanged for the 'Aldie' property. Mercer never married.

In November 1811, U. S. Postmaster General Gideon Granger authorized the post office called Aldie, and Peyton Cooke became the first postmaster, holding the position until 1829, when Edmund Tyler took over. He held the position through 1844, followed by two short-timers. Then in 1854, Elizabeth Stover became one of Loudoun's first postmistresses.

PHOTO COURTESY LOUDOUN COUNTY DEPT. OF PLANNING

Post Office, Aldie, circa 1811

Aldie made its first separate appearance in the U. S. Census of 1820, with 248 residents. The town, only ten years old, was the fourth largest in the county, next to Leesburg, Waterford, and Middleburg. In the next census year, 1830, Aldie had 260 persons, among whom 132 were slaves. Then the population began declining, in part because of the prominence of nearby Middleburg, which had been incorporated in 1831. Additionally, Middleburg's leading entrepreneur, Noble Beveridge, had its two grand buildings, now the Red Fox Inn and Windsor House, built in 1827.

Aldie's heyday of some two decades was largely due to the mill's installation of Oliver Evans's belt-driven machinery complex. Mr. Evans, an Ellicott City, Maryland, miller and inventor, had patented a mechanical system that ground and moved the grain and meal from start to finish with little manual labor, and Mercer took out a license to use Oliver Evans's inventions. During this era, Aldie was also the head of two new turnpikes along the routes of the old Belhaven and Mountain Roads—the Ashby's Gap Turnpike, complete with the 1813 stone bridge to Middleburg that year; and the Aldie and Snickers' Gap Turnpike (Snickersville Pike), complete to the gap by 1818.

Charles Fenton Mercer, occupied with politics and other business concerns, leased his half-share of the mill operations to William Noland, the sawmill operator, who also served in the general assembly with Captain Mercer. In 1810, Mr. Noland and James Barbour of Orange County were co-authors of the act creating the Virginia Literary Fund to pay for the first public schools "for the poor in any county of the state." William Noland's annual rents to C. F. Mercer for the sawmill and gristmill totaled $2,000 one year, more than five times the average wage. William Cooke sold his share of the milling business to Mr. Mercer for $11,250 in 1816. Until C. F. Mercer sold the mill to townsman Captain John Moore in 1835, he continued leasing the mill and its outbuildings to various tenants. An 1822 newspaper ad notes that "the largest flour manufactory in the county" will be leased in July, containing "Merchant, Grist, Plaster, & Saw" operations, with granary, store, and dwelling house. The lessee was Asa Rogers, owner of the nearby Sally Mill. The lessees from 1824 to 1829 were the Hixson brothers, owners of the Dover Mill.

Photo courtesy Loudoun Co. Dept. of Planning

The big wheels at Aldie

Elected a U. S. Congressman in 1817, Charles Fenton Mercer served eleven terms. On the national level he championed free public education, suppression of the slave trade, and the colonization in Africa for freed slaves. With his commercial enterprises and public service out of the way, in 1845 he wrote *An Exposition of the Weakness and Inefficiency of the Government of the United States.* As first president of the Chesapeake and Ohio Canal Company in 1828, he served as chief executive until the canal was complete to Harper's Ferry in 1833. He had a decided monetary interest in the success of the canal, for it was to link with the proposed Goose Creek Canal in Loudoun County, where one of its three destinations was to be the Aldie Mill. Mr. Mercer financed the survey for the Goose Creek Canal and paid for the lock on the C & O Canal that would eventually allow flatboats to cross from Goose Creek. The canal never reached Aldie, stopping some six miles short at Evergreen Mills.

Turning to Charles Fenton Mercer's village, its first church was a Free or Union Church, to be used specifically by four denominations. It had been completed by November, 1848, and its deed noted "building erected thereon...to be used as a house of public Worship for...Methodist, Baptist, Presbyterians and Episcopalians." The one-acre lot, donated by William and Catharine Noland of Middleburg, could also hold a graveyard. During the Civil War, the building was used as a hospital, and there were several interments. In the late 1950s a mower of the grown-over churchyard, thinking the unmarked gravestones were just stones, removed many. Some were lined up against the trees; others now lie buried in the grass.

Illustration courtesy Thomas Balch Library

Union sentry at Aldie, 1863

Of Aldie businesses in pre-Civil War years, it is known that Alexander Moore, son of Alexandrian John Moore, who bought the Aldie Mill in 1835, was in partnership with his father at the mill's store by the late 1850s. After the May 23, 1861, vote to determine whether Virginia should secede from the Union, the dissenting voters' names were recited, as was customary. John Moore had voted "no," and his son, Alexander, had voted "yes." The Aldie precinct vote was 54 for secession; 5 against.

The onset of June 1863, saw running cavalry actions along the

Ashby's Gap Turnpike; the Union staging ground was at Aldie. It was at the diZerega place (now the Briar Patch) that General Alfred Pleasanton's forces first encountered severe resistance. Ellen Tyler, living at the house later to become the Episcopal Rectory, remembered that the Union officer, ready to charge the enemy, hidden behind haystacks, yelled, "I'll take this hill if I have to lose every damned man I have." She was not surprised at his zeal, but she was shocked that he should say the word "damned." He lost quite a few men, but he took the hill. After the sides regrouped, General Pleasanton decided that he should push west at "all costs." On June 21 a Union patrol reached the top of the Blue Ridge and determined that Lee was moving northward—to Gettysburg.

Later in the war, when one of the many Yankee patrols to pass through Aldie spotted a horse grazing in the back field, Ellen Tyler told the patroller her husband was a doctor and needed the horse for his calls. Edwin Andrew Tyler was actually a furniture maker, and he also served in the Confederate Army.

Partisan Ranger John Singleton Mosby was responsible for two remembered Aldie affairs. The first on March 2, 1863, after Union forces had captured several Middleburg citizens, many quite elderly, and had walked them east toward their lines in Fairfax County. Mosby had just entered Middleburg, and noting the "tears and lamentations of the daughters…Their beauty had won the hearts of many of my men," he decided to pursue the Federal cavalry with 17 men. Escorting the hostages was a rear guard of 60, they were ridden down by Mosby's Rangers at the Aldie Mill. To escape, some jumped into the wheat bins "and buried themselves like rats." Others jumped into the hoppers "and came near being ground up into flour." Captain Mosby mused, "To avenge the wrongs of the distressed damsels is one of the vows of knighthood."

In April, 1864, Aldie's John Alexander, who rode with Mosby, recalled:

> The turnpike makes a sharp bend around the spur of the mountain and at once crosses Little River over one of those narrow stone bridges. The enemy would have to cross it four abreast. As the Yankees bolted around the mountain and across the bridge, Mosby charged them.

At the close of the war, German immigrant George Bodmer, who came to America to escape conscription into the army, built the still-standing stone and frame wheelwright and buggy-manufacturing shop, one of the finest survivors of its kind, just east of Little River and north of the pike. In 1869 he built his house next door. He ran the complex until the 20th century, when the shop was taken over by his son, John W. Bodmer. When the Ford motor people offered John the agency for all of Loudoun County, he refused, saying, "The auto will never amount to anything." His shop went out of business about 1930.

PHOTO COURTESY LOUDOUN CO. DEPT. OF PLANNING

Bodmer's wheelwright shop

This area across Little River was soon called Georgetown, a verbal play on Washington, D. C.'s Georgetown, across Rock Creek from the capital city.

Aldie had five general stores in the 1870s, and of long-time merchants there was Marshall A. Carter, in business through the early 20th century. His brick store and house stood three houses west of Partlow's and was torn down in 1928. The bricks were used by Paul Ferguson to build his house, now stuccoed. Captain John R. Hutchison, in business with his wife, Laura, had a store just west of the old post office recently restored for Tucker Withers. The store burned in 1914. John T. Laws's store was open until the mid-1890s, taken over by John W. Hensley at the turn of the century. This store often held the post office until it burned in March, 1929. Just east of Aldie, on the south side of the pike, by the stone house, once the Redd place and later the Moore place, Joseph S. Redd had a store that sold liquor through the 1880s. John P. Green had a store until the early 1880s; its location is not known.

There were also two to three physicians practicing in town during the 1870s and '80s, with Thomas L. Laws and George A. Quimby the leading practitioners. Dr. Quimby also farmed, and Dr. Samuel Simpson, an 1880s physician, farmed and also was postmaster, 1881-1886. The oldest remembered doctor, Ira H. Thomas, served as druggist and dentist as well, with his first office in a building long gone, just west of the Little River Inn. In 1914 he moved to the back of the present "Little River" antiques shop. He practiced from the late 1880s until about 1920.

Dr. Charles Goettling came in from Middleburg about that time, with deserved laurels from his round-the-clock ministering during the 1918 and 1919 flu epidemics. By 1922 he added a front section and put in a soda fountain, but a few years later lost his license for setting up a still in the pharmacy. His wife, Lucy, and daughter, Louise, then ran the drug store for a while, and it ended its days as Ashton Tavenner's store, a Depression casualty.

Of the Aldie Mill, after John Moore's death, Alexander Moore ran the mill in early 1880s. His nephew, James E. Douglass, brought from Alexandria to escape the Union occupation during the war, followed John Moore about 1884. His son, John Moore Douglass, assumed part ownership in the mid-teens, and his son, James Moore Douglass began partnering with his father in 1945.

As had been the custom in colonial times, the miller kept his toll, generally one-sixth of the initially weighed corn and one-eighth of the wheat. James Moore Douglass would tell this tale:

> The miller asked the boy tolling the grain. "Whose wheat is that?"
> "Mr. Fairfax's, sir."
> "Did you toll him?"
> "Yes, sir."
> "Well, toll him again; he's a rich man and can afford it."
> The next day the miller again came upon the boy tolling the grain. "Whose corn meal is that?"
> "Mr. Jones's, sir."
> "Did you toll him?"
> "Yes, sir."
> "Well, toll him again; he's a poor man, let's keep him poor."

In reality, the Aldie millers were as kind as local bankers used to be, for the mills were public utilities and were required by law not to turn away a customer. The Douglasses can show you a linen-bound account book of 1830 recording a cash loan of five dollars to debt-ridden former President James Monroe.

Of other businesses, Dulaney Bruin was the saddle and harness maker and tanner, from the late 1880s through the early 1920s. Sanford Gulick Jr., then converted the building to a store, until it became another Depression casualty. The establishment still stands northeast of the fire house. To its west, and torn down in 1969, when the fire house arose, was Edward B. Goode's blacksmith and agricultural implements shop, active from the mid-1890s to the early 1930s. Ed's son, Willie

Goode, operated the Aldie Garage from the late '30s through the late '40s. To the harness shop's east on the site of John Hutchison's burnt store, Ira 'Iry' Carter built a store. He also plied a huckster wagon through the Bull Run Mountain country. Carter's store went out of business in the late 1930s; it's now an antique shop. Just east of George Bodmer's house, in a square building by the road, a Dr. Metzger had an apothecary at the turn of the 19th century.

West of Little River, Edwin Andrew Tyler ran his furniture-making shop with steam-powered lathes behind the present Little River Inn. He was in business through the early 1900s, helped by his son, William E. Tyler, who took over the works. William was also the town magistrate, undertaker, and a roofer during the 20th century's first two decades. Just east of the inn, by the road, was a small building that served as a sometime post office, and in the 1920s through 1940s as the office of the Loudoun-Prince William Telephone Company. Olivia Ambler ran the switchboard and was on duty from 7 a.m. to 9 p.m. She got $29 a month for her services, plus free phone calls. Both of these buildings stood until about 1960. Aldie also had from one to two "hotels," as the gazetteers called them, in the 1880s and '90s. In reality they were probably boarding houses, run by John S. Laws and later John F. Simpson, and William B. Carter. Their locations are uncertain.

PHOTO COURTESY LOUDOUN CO. DEPT. OF PLANNING

One of Tucker Withers's restorations, Little River Inn

The pre-1954 corner of the Snickersville and Ashby's Gap Turnpikes was known as Tollhouse Corner, for its two tollhouses. The one for the Ashby Gap pike appears to have disappeared during the Civil War, but the one for the Snickersville Pike still stands. In the early years of this century Asbury Allen lived there, and his blacksmith shop stood about 300 feet northwest of the corner.

During the summers of 1913-1914, an Italian road crew laid a one-lane macadamized road seven miles from Mount Zion Church west to Middleburg. To pay for the paving, new tollhouses were set up at the east end of both Middleburg and Aldie, opposite the Methodist Church. The tolls, 3¢ for a horse, 6¢ for a buggy, and 30¢ for an auto, were removed in 1919 when the state took over the road's maintenance.

The Aldie Methodist Church joined the old Free Church in 1884, the 5,900-square-foot lot having been bought for $20 from merchant John P. Green and his wife, Mary, the previous September. Warrenton contractor, William J. Hanback, brick-veneered the front and added the steeple in 1970. That same year Landmark contractor Hugh Griffith added the rear wing. The Episcopal Church of Our Redeemer was built in 1895, the quarter-acre lot having been donated from a corner of Oak Hill farm by owner Henry Fairfax in 1890. In March, two years later, the Presbyterians bought the Free Church from its trustees and wasted no time in tearing down the old brick building and building the present frame one, dedicated November 20, 1892.

As one of Loudoun's larger villages—population 170 or so in the late 19th century and 160 in the early 20th—the stuccoed-frame schoolhouse on Meetinghouse Lane had two rooms. It dates from the early 1870s and was built with funds raised from horse meets and steeplechases held on the present elementary-school grounds. Because of the large stovepipes that wound their way through the room—pipes still visible as they penetrate the roof—everyone called the building Stove Pipe Academy. The last word would give the school name a bit of respectability, as many old Virginia public schools were termed academies and even colleges.

Stove Pipe closed in 1914, and in its confines Robert Lee Bodmer ran a Maxwell auto agency for a few years. As he was a big shipper from The Plains railroad station he had a discount yearly toll rate and was always waived through by the toll keepers. Thus his nephew, John Perry Bodmer, found a way to get some money to buy candy. John P., the son of wagon-maker John W. Bodmer, often drove a two-horse wagon to The Plains, and his father would give him 16 cents for tolls—8¢ to 'Bush' Nichols at Aldie and 8¢ to Frank Saunders at Middleburg. The toll keepers, thinking that John P. was Robert's son, waved him through. John bought his candy for a while, but then fessed up and told his father. When the tollgates closed in 1919, Frank and Nellie Saunders moved to Aldie and for many years raised bees.

Stove Pipe Academy was replaced by the frame, eight-room Aldie

High School and elementary school in 1915, the land bought and the structure built by private subscriptions. As Lincoln High School was known for its scholars, Aldie High was known for its boys' and girls' basketball teams and boys' baseball teams. This tradition stemmed from second principal Charles K. Brown of the Unison area. He loved athletics and was an organizer.

At the school grounds in July, another sport, jousting, was the big event at the Aldie Community Fair. The area was filled with Model Ts as people came to see horse races, stock-judging competitions, and to hear the Leesburg Band. The jousting tournaments, last to be held in Loudoun County, ended when the last fair was held in 1925.

Next year the present six-room school arose–by now the population had dropped to 130–and in 1938 the frame agricultural annex arose, built partially with federal funds. Ruth Ferguson Tyler filled in for the agricultural instructor who had just been drafted. She was of the old school–a disciplinarian, attentive to the basics, and a strong grammarian. She stayed for 24 years, often teaching the fourth grade. Another fondly remembered teacher is Sue Kirk Lipps, who taught from 1943-1966. Aldie High's last class graduated in 1954, and that fall busing began to the new Loudoun County High School in Leesburg. In 1964

PHOTO COURTESY THOMAS BALCH LIBRARY

The 'rescued' Little River stone bridge, Aldie

next-door old Aldie High was demolished.

Years 1928 and 1929 brought in the modern era. Route 50 was finally paved from Aldie to Middleburg, but gone in its stead were a beautiful stone-arch bridge across the mill's tail race and two historical markers, one memorializing the June, 1863, cavalry battle; the other, erroneously, the route of the Braddock Road (actually Route 9). The highway department also wanted to replace the 1813 double-arch stone bridge across Little River. The widow of State Senator Henry Fairfax, Eugenia Fairfax, literally, so I'm told, stood in front of the bulldozers to save the span. In raising the road level to meet the bridge, road workers created an embankment that would back up flood waters and nearly submerge the Aldie Mill and adjacent buildings.

Arthur G. Jackson quickly responded to the paving, opening his stuccoed Texaco station with brick portico. Competitor Samuel Preston Luck, who operated the Standard Oil station in Middleburg, then put a sign atop his building, "All die five miles." Jackson ran his station until the mid-1950s, when his son, Guy Jackson, took over. Louis Watson Carter, who had opened his next-door Aldie Garage in 1958, consolidated both concerns about 1965. Louis's son, Louis Wayne Carter Jr., has been running the business since 1974.

PHOTO COURTESY LOUDOUN DEPT. OF PLANNING

Formerly Jackson's Texaco

In March 1929, the 'big store,' once John Hensley's and now trading as Goode and Furr, burned to the ground. The fire had broken out at 4:30 a.m. The next morning the safe was found ajar with $500 missing. The case remains unsolved. A month before, Murrel Partlow had purchased Ed Goode's building and Murrel asked Ed Goode whether he was going to rebuild. E. B. said "No." Murrel had no intention of opening a store, but as the downstairs where Murrel lived had recently been Will Carter's store–Will had competed, unsuccessfully with his brother, Iry–he took a chance. Seven months later the stock market crashed, but Partlow's would be the village's one Depression survivor, partly due to moving the post office there. Samuel Thornton Ish was postmaster then, and held the job until 1957.

Murrel Partlow usually leased the business, but after two lessees failed he came back to take over the store himself in 1935. Up went a sign, courtesy of Coca Cola, reading "M. Partlow"; below was the perennial bottle. There were now two Gulf pumps outside, and his gas and Arthur Jackson's was down to 10¢ a gallon. He again leased the business when sugar was rationed–in 1942. His son, Murrel Lee Partlow, bought the store in 1951, and with his wife, Lillian Robertson Partlow, ran "Partlow's Grocery" until 1983. Since then he had leased it out for two years when it was called "The Village Market." Under lessees Dwight, James, and John Beiler, it has held the name "Aldie Country Store" since 1985. Of the three, today John Beiler remains behind the counter

Hunt Country traffic to the steeplechases and race meets in the Middleburg area prompted the opening of Mercer Tavern, at the southeast corner of the pike and Meetinghouse Lane, in 1939. Emily diZerega and Jack York ran Mercer's through World War II, and they featured good country food, beer, and a jukebox. When it closed, R. R. Ralph opened up a beer hall and sandwich shop in Dulaney Bruin's old saddlery in the Georgetown section of the village. It lasted until the early 1950s. Mercer Tavern became a "Fresh Fruit from Florida" stand after the war, and then the grocery store of Frank Flippo, brother of Roy Flippo, who opened Leesburg's Laurel Brigade Inn in 1949. Frank also closed in the early 1950s. Antiques have taken over—and nearly everywhere else.

Talk about a fire company had been bantered about for several years, but in the spring of 1955, Frederick L. "Fritz" Hutchison, who had been away teaching, decided to organize a meeting in the Aldie School Agricultural Building. That September, with $5,500 raised from auctions, turkey shoots, "women-less weddings," pancake suppers, and a carnival, the town bought a 1939 Chevrolet 500-gallon pumper. It was first housed in Arthur Jackson's garage. Then the company bought Willie Goode's garage. It was torn down in 1969, when the present fire hall was built. The first pumper served the Aldie Volunteer Fire Department through 1971. Concern about getting men to the right bank of the Little River, in case something happened to the stone bridge, led to the construction of the foot bridge just south of the stone span, in the fall of 1982. The prime mover was the Aldie Ruritan Club. Their walkway provides a close-up view of the 1813 span and access from the Aldie Mill to Indian Spring, a rock-lined bowl sequestered among the hemlocks along the Little River.

Aldie's other new building is the 1960 brick post office, opened by Postmaster Franklin W. Payne, successor in 1957 at Partlow's to Samuel Ish. F. W. Payne remained until 1986, when Sue Cornelius took over.

Tucker Withers, who opened the Little River Inn in June, 1982, has, with his various restoration projects, been largely responsible for the perking up of Aldie during the 1980s. He had originally planned to move from Maryland to live in Middleburg, but while waiting for his realtor, ex-marine Mickey Finn, at his Mercer Tavern office, Mr. Withers encountered Ralph Cockerill, who looked him in the eye and asked him if he weren't the son of Cleve Withers. Tucker said "Yes," and Ralph proceeded to tell Tucker how he and his father had palled around years ago. Tucker had never known that his father had Aldie roots, and so he came to live in the old hometown.

John Moore Douglass joined his father in the milling business about 1915. It was he who stopped grinding flour in the early 1930s. The mill's big year was 1946, as all the farms were expanding after World War II, and none yet had the machinery to grind feed. James Edward 'Ned' Douglass, John Moore's nephew, then ran the mill. As farmers bought their own portable grinding mills, Douglass increased the sales of corn meal to local stores. About 1955 the Mediterranean Fly got into the meal and nearly half of it had to be returned. That year the upper wheel stopped grinding, and about 1964 the lower wheel wore out. Douglass asked the Fitz Company, who had installed the wheels about 1900, how much it would cost to replace them. The estimate was $10,000, so it was cheaper for Ned to buy a tractor to run the machinery. The mill stopped selling feed in 1971. When interviewed in 1977, Ned said, "Mills were built to shake from their noise, and when the noise stops they collapse from the stillness."

Ned and his wife, Sarah Love Douglass, did not let this happen, for in 1981 they donated the mill and its grounds to the Virginia Outdoors Foundation. The VOF began restoring the building, its works, and the dam and mill race. Financing to the tune of two million dollars came largely from an anonymous benefactor, who I suspect was Paul Mellon. The mill was slated to open "each next year," but the health department feared that if the race were filled with water, nine septic systems would backup. So, they didn't issue a permit until 1999, and "next year" finally came that year.

PHOTO COURTESY LOUDOUN COUNTY DEPT. OF PLANNING

Restored and renovated Aldie Mill today

Upperville

"A Mile Long, An Inch Wide"
–Kitty Slater

There are two images of this village, one, the traditional northern Piedmont row town along the Ashby's Gap Turnpike, its old homes topped by perennial end chimneys; two, the gathering place of that select echelon of foxhunters. Kitty Slater, chronicler of the Hunt Country calls them "Cliff-dwellers."

Writer John Updike might have agreed. He coined this four-liner in 1961:

In Upperville the upper crust
Say, 'Bottoms up!' from dawn to dusk.
And 'Ups-a-daisy, dear!' at will
I want to live in Upper-ville.

The village of 350 sits on 3,000 acres granted to the Reverend Charles Green in 1742. Green was the rector of Truro Parish, which then included Fairfax and the future Loudoun County. He was a man of the world in more than the sense of owning vast acreages. He was accused by Colonel William Washington of having tried to seduce his bride, the former Ann Fairfax, other similar indiscretions, defrauding people out of property, refusing to baptize dangerously ill children, and illegally affixing the religious preference to the tax roles of every person in his parish. Green, of course—was not of Upperville. He lived in eastern Loudoun.

The parson sold his 3,000 acres in 1763 to Joseph Allen and John Violett, and within the next two generations the tract was broken up into parcels bought by the progenitors of the old families: Josiah Suttle, Stephen McPherson, Joseph Carr, Joseph Gibson.

By 1790, Joseph Carr had a mill built on Pantherskin Creek, and within a few years opened a still-standing store beside the mill. With a couple of other houses and undoubtedly a blacksmith shop on his 108 acres at the west end of town, the Carr-financed community became known as Carr Town–a name used on maps through the Civil War.

Carr Town prospered because of its location along the Belhaven Road, that forerunner of the Ashby's Gap Turnpike. The road was well-traveled, as noted by a November 1786 petition from Loudouners stating the road "has now become very publick & so cut by the Waggons…it require much labour to keep it fit for use." As each county was then responsible for the road's upkeep in their county, Loudoun said the road was in Fauquier and vice versa. The state then told both counties to stop quibbling and to take turns keeping the road "in repair…as within their county as without."

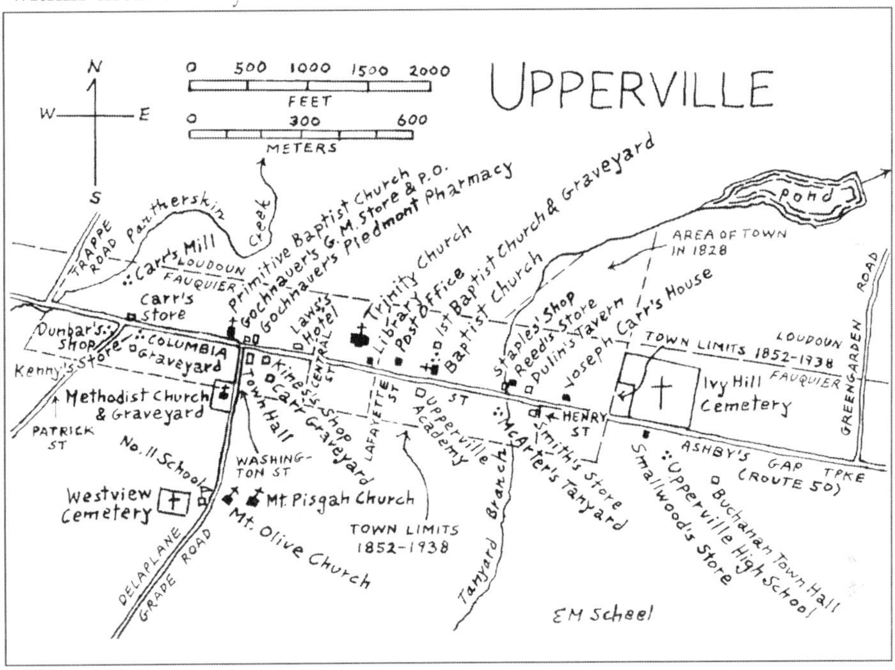

Even a toll gate at Alexandria, authorized by Virginia's General Assembly in October 1785, couldn't supply enough funds to keep the busy road in repair. Soon, both Loudoun and Fauquier citizens were complaining that they, who lived within three miles of the road–now the first toll road in the United States–shouldn't have to work six days a year to keep the road passable, especially since Frederick and Berkeley County wagons were doing the damage. Normally, each county adult male was required to work the roads one or two days a year–a law until 1894. Regarding the complaint the state did nothing.

But Carr Towners managed, and the wagoners' stopping and trading brought prosperity and a post office. Joseph Carr was not a vain man. Even though Carr Town had been in use for almost 20 years, when the first post office opened its doors in 1807, the name was Upperville. The name's origin may have come from the usage of "Lower

Town," for Carr Town, and "Upper Town," for the higher elevations of the east end of town where Joseph Carr lived. He wanted no part of his businesses during non-working hours.

Perhaps the one drawback to his home's location–or maybe it was a plus–was the tavern of John Dulin, 300 feet away. Dulin's was built about 1789, and until 1811 it was the main town stopover on the old Belhaven Road. That year Dr. Thomas W. Smith bought Dulin's, converted it into his home and office, and also operated a store in the frame-encased log building across the street.

Upperville may also have alluded to the naming of Middleburg, with the newer town the "upper" ville between Winchester and Alexandria. So, when in 1819 the Virginia General Assembly gave its meaningless charter to the village, the act read:

> "30 acres of land, the property of Joseph Carr at a place called Upperville, in the County of Loudoun."

The location will surprise many today, but until George Love surveyed the Loudoun-Fauquier line in 1824, Upperville was considered part of Loudoun County. And while Mr. Love changed all that by shifting the line about 1,500 feet to the north, as late as 1835 gazetteers were placing the town in Loudoun County. And that's where Yardley Taylor thought it was when he rode down Columbia Street and counted 64 dwellings "not more than 200 yards from the Fauquier line." Today there are not many more and, as in yesteryear, they stood-on 54 lots, platted, appropriately, by George Love in 1828. To avoid controversy, though, surveyor Love declined to show the new county boundary on his new map.

Mr. Taylor's description of the town, undoubtedly garnered with help from a friendly postmaster, spoke to a good bit of bustle along the Ashby Gap Turnpike, the town's Columbia Street. Except for Berry's Ferry across the Shenandoah, one could bounce along in relative comfort all the way from Aldie, where the pike began, to Winchester. The last barrier, Goose Creek, was broached by the stone bridge in 1818. The postmaster counted three stores, two taverns, one hotel (not Dulins, for that house had become the home of the first town doctor Thomas W. Smith), Carr's Mill, which then ground flour and was about to have a new owner, Joseph Gibson, three churches with one under construction, an academy, a hatter, tanner, shoemaker, saddler, bricklayer, tinner, and two millwrights, stone masons, plasterers, and finished carpenters.

The population was 300 (times haven't changed) and included an attorney and two physicians.

Editor Joseph Martin, when reading Yardley Taylor's description, did not doubt the veracity of his words, but wondered if Taylor knew where he was. In the *Gazetteer of Virginia*, where the words later appear, is this footnote after the name Upperville: "This post village has by some accident got transposed—it ought to have been in Fauquier Co."

The four churches have been long gone, some destroyed, some just taken down. In three cases new buildings mark their sites. The Primitive Baptists built first, with their Lower Goose Creek Church having dated from 1805. Appropriately the building was located in "Lower Town" reinforcing that name. A new church, in the style of Loudoun's Ketoctin and Mount Zion, and Fauquier's Thumb Run and Pleasant Vale arose in 1844, and the present plastered-frame structure was built in 1897. The 1844 church was just getting on in years, so it was taken down.

Methodists built next, on a Washington Street lot donated by George and Elizabeth Calvert. The year was 1832, but during the war, when the building served as a hospital, errant shells broke through roof and walls. Using much of the old wall brick and the design of the 1832 structure, the Methodists rededicated their building in November 1869.

In 1833, following the Regular Baptists split with their brethren, the brick Baptist Church arose on the east end of town. At least that's what the church history says. But why didn't Yardley Taylor mention that church? Probably because the church was founded in 1833, and the building arose a few years later. While it survived the war, structural damage set in during the following decade, and the building was replaced in 1889. Its elaborate open bell tower and Star of David gable window reflect the architectural tastes of pastor Isaac Beverly Lake, who also had noted painter Lucien Powell decorate the apses of Ketoctin and Ebenezer Churches with *trompe l'oeil* motifs (fooling the eye so the flat surface appears three dimensional). The Reverend Lake shepherded these churches for a half century, from 1872–1922.

Concord Free Meetinghouse was standing prior to Mr. Taylor's visit, and until the Fauquier-Loudoun Bank arose about 1920, the old meeting stood on that lot. The bank, a victim of mismanagement, as was a short-lived counterpart, circa 1905, closed in 1928. In its stead came the post office, opened at the building in 1935.

The Episcopal Church under construction was in that state until 1842, and, in turn, was replaced by a frame structure in 1895. That building became a memory in 1955, when work began on present Trinity Church, built in five years largely through gifts of parishioner Paul Mellon. The church and adjoining complex, designed by H. Page Cross in the style of a 12th-century French country church, sits in harmony amidst architecture that is anything but 12th-century or French. Robert Hancock was the master builder and in 1960 put in place the bronze weathercock covered with gold leaf. The Cock was the ancient symbol of St. Peter, and predates the cross as the usual ornament for Episcopal

PHOTO COURTESY LOUDOUN COUNTY DEPT. OF PLANNING

Trinity Epicopal Church, Upperville

Churches in pre-19th-century Europe and America.

Upperville Academy, the institution of learning mentioned by Yardley Taylor, was opened by Dr. Bushrod Rust just about the time Mr. Taylor came through town.From about 1840 until the war, the school was run by James J. Armstrong, an excellent teacher and strict disciplinarian. Commissioned a captain in the Civil War, Armstrong was killed at Vicksburg, the first engagement he fought in. Tuition at the school in 1836 was $93 a year with two weeks off for spring vacation. Board ran $52.

Businessmen in town during its early years were John Byrne and members of the McCarter (McArtor) family, operators of the tanyard on the branch by that name. William H. May, later Alexandria's leading hardware merchant, received his training at this tanyard known for decades as McCarter's. Then, on the west end of town, old "Lower Town," Amos Pierce had the blacksmith shop. Thomas Dunbar was the main carpenter and coffin maker and Harrison Lunsford the shoemaker. In the center of town Jonas Gore had his blacksmith shop. Exact locations can be read from Curtis Chappelear's notes about town in his posthumously published *Maps and Notes of Upper Fauquier County.*

C. W. Pembroke Gochnauer (locally pronounced Gof'nour) ran the main general mercantile store in prewar years. He opened for business about 1840, and his brick building with frame front stands next to the late Gochnauer Drug Store. During much of the 19th century the Upperville Post Office was located in Pembroke Gochnauer's store. It was that family who campaigned strongly for the town's incorporation, a reality in 1852.

PHOTO COURTESY LOUDUN CO. DEPT. ECON. DEV.
Today's Post Office, Upperville

A word about the street names that first appear on George Love's 1828 survey. Columbia Street, today's Rt. 50, and the turnpike of old took its name from the word Columbia that was used to describe the new United States. By the 1820s Columbia was a popular figure, appearing as a stately woman dressed in flowing garments and bearing an American Flag. Flanking side streets, today's Trappe Road and a short lane just east of Tanyard Branch, were Patrick and Henry Streets. The middle side streets were Washington (today's Delaplane Grade Road to Delaplane), Lafayette, and an unrelated Central. In all, the street names speak to a celebration of liberty and the manifest destiny of the country to reach America's western shores.

Upperville along with all of the Ashby Gap Turnpike from the gap east to Aldie was the scene of nearly one continually shifting cavalry maneuver and engagement from June 17-21, 1863, as both armies vied for position or route to Gettysburg. Most of the town's buildings were spared because the soldiers, suspecting sharpshooters in windows, avoided riding on Columbia Street.

One Civil War casualty yet visible is the ruined Carr's Mill, burned November 29, 1864, on orders from Major General Phillip H. Sheridan. The mill was possibly the first to see the torch following Sheridan's order: "You will consume and destroy all forage and subsistence, burn all barns and mills, and their contents..." And while other mills within a few miles of Upperville were rebuilt, Carr's was not. And Upperville slept more soundly.

At the turn of the century there were two public schools in Upperville. A frame two-story elementary and high school stood just east of the Primitive Baptist Church. The high school was open until 1925, when it was replaced by the brick Upperville High. That last town school burned about 1980.

Upperville High in the late 1930s and early '40s gained fame in the athletic world for its boys' basketball teams. Coach William Tyler, the principal, sometimes stretched eligibility a bit by having the better players from Unison-Bloomfield and Aldie Highs join the team late into the season—especially if Upperville had a shot at winning the state championship. Someone, maybe coach Tyler, paid the $10-or-so fee it cost to let a Loudouner attend the Fauquier school.

The black community, faithful servants to the scions of Columbia Street families, centered their churches and schools on south Washington Street. There you can still see the plastered-frame No. 11 School built 1899, closed 1949. In Fauquier, schools for black children were numbered as were schools for white children. This custom differed from the normal Virginia practice of lettering black schools. In Fauquier, too, several schools were always known by their number and never had names. Across the street from No. 11 stand the black churches; Mount Pisgah Baptist, organized in 1877, built in 1900, and Mount Olive Methodist, built in 1909.

Upperville had three main stores in postwar years, roughly 1880 through 1925. In the center of town Preston Brooke Gochnauer had the big general-merchandise store, and was in partnership with his brother, C. W. Gochnauer, who specialized in stoves and tinware. Nearly opposite that store was James Abner Johnston's. Jim had started out in town as a saddler in the 1880s. In the same building Blanche Haley, the milliner, specialized in fancy hats. She stopped sewing in the mid-1920s.

About 1933, when 3.2 percent beer became legal in Virginia, Jim's son, always known as "Bee," ran a beer parlor there for a decade or so.

By Tanyard Branch in the Upper Town, Thomas Reed's store dates from 1895. His father, William P. Reed, had run the blacksmith shop next door since about 1880, and then went into the general-mercantile business about 1889 in an earlier store. A.Cook Reed followed his father Thomas Reed. In1919, Ernest Fleming, who had clerked in the store, took over and continued its old name "A. C. Reed's," until 1974. The store remains open, trading as the Upperville Country Store.

When Reed's (actually operated by Ernest Fleming) was going strong, the store was open from six in the morning until nine at night. The drive-in-for-gas portico was added in 1923 to celebrate the paving of Columbia Street. Added traffic then prompted his brother Fred's garage across the street. The garage closed in 1966. The west end also had its garage, run during the same era by Howard Lucius, at the site of the present well-drilling enterprise. Mr. Lucius's garage was open until the late 1940s.

Next door to Reed's Store, straddling Tanyard Branch, Howard Staples and Charles Wiltshire had their blacksmith shop. It was not uncommon for smiths to locate shops over a small creek; all they had to do was drop the hot waste metal through a hole in the floor. Wiltshire left in the teens to start his own blacksmith shop opposite Charlie Kenny's west-end store. He ran it through 1935. Staples now concentrated on wheelwright work and closed the shop in the late 1920s. Wiltshire also had run an undertaking establishment since early in the century. He had learned the trade from Thomas S. Dunbar, a coffin-maker, wheelwright, and coach-and-wagon maker of the 1880s–1890s.

A fourth store in post-1920 years was C. T. "Charlie" Scott's, located in the brick building just east of Pembroke S. Gochnauer's Piedmont Pharmacy. Several others ran Scott's until Irvin Wiley closed up in the late 1960s. At the pharmacy, famed for its soda fountain, Pembroke didn't handle prescriptions, leaving them for brother Fred Gochnauer, the doctor. Pembroke, called "Brooke," was too busy carrying the mail into Fauquier and up along the Blue Ridge, to Llangollen and Blakeley Grove. Joe Gibson was the other carrier, his route led up Willisville to the Trappe.

Vergie Gibson Gochnauer, Pembroke's daughter-in-law, was often behind the counter in the twenties through thirties, and from 1936,

Photo courtesy Anne Slater Coyner

Looking west from Gochnauer Pharmacy, ca. 1910

on Cornelia Carver's presence changed the name to Carver's Drug Store. She and husband James O'Hara owned the business from 1953 until it closed in 1993. Since 1924, buses from the west and Washington have stopped in front of the building– first Virginia Transit, then Greyhound and Trailways.

Gochnauer's store also changed purpose in 1931, when Dr. Fred's daughter, Anne, and her friend Julia Gatewood, opened their Golden Horseshoe Antique Shop and Tea Room. "Luncheon and Tea every day except Sunday," as they advertised, lasted but a few years. The antique shop, under the same name, goes on.

Four town physicians served long terms. Samuel Edward Gulick was the doctor from the late 1860s until about 1900. When asked if he served in the Civil War, he replied, "I was trained to save life, not to take it." From 1885 until his death at 48 in1907, Charles Frederick Rinker cared for the town. Then Fred Gochnauer was town physician from 1904-1945, and would have been there longer had it not been for a bit of fatal irony. In Winchester Hospital for routine gall bladder surgery, Dr. Gochnauer died on the operating table. He was 66. An obituary noted "he was a physician for all classes and races." Dr. Charles W. Warren, who had just received his army discharge, took over. With time out for war, he had practised in town since 1936. His retirement in

1978 marked the end of the Upperville physicians. A pricey area and village was not the place for a young doctor.

Since Upperville was a pretty healthy place, the doctors' main job was to repair sprained limbs of riders and foxhunters and to deliver babies. In the latter task they were always helped by black "mid-mothers," as midwives in the Upperville area were called. They looked after the new mother and baby for about a week and charged $2 or $3 other than their room and board. The town's Hattie Bayliss and Rectortown's Winnie White are two who are remembered.

Across the street, on the pike's south side, Forrest Rhodes, assisted by Homer Pearson, had a store from the thirties through the fifties, and before 1914 this building was the town hall. Here the corporation met and dancing and theatricals held sway on weekends. In 1914, General James Buchanan, who lived at Ayrshire north of town, funded the greater part of a building known as the Buchanan Town Hall. The town officers then moved into the building, but only for four years, as Upperville then gave up its incorporated status. As all town minutes are lost, old-timers can only vaguely recall a lack of interest.

Then, in 1937, Upperville reincorporated, but only until the following year, when a brouhaha arose over a proposed town water system. As most folk were on wells, they opposed the system and again voted to disband the corporation. However, during that one incorporated season, the town garnered enough funds to lay a concrete sidewalk on the pike's north side.

One business east of Buchanan Hall worth noting is Francis Smallwood's still-going combined eatery, gas station, and home, built 1925 by and for Mr. Smallwood. He had noticed that youngsters at the high school, once next door, had a penchant for soda pop and fast food. And as it was on the edge of town, the eatery also attracted foxhunters and horseback riders. In 1982, I noted that Mary and Henry Houchin had run the concern since 1960.

When foxhunters wanted to deck out, they stopped at J. Shirley Kines's. Shirley Kines's tailor shop was to Upperville as Charlie Osburn's saddlery was to Unison. If you were decked out in Kines's finery you were in the upper echelon. He and his older brother Fitzhugh "Fitz" Kines ran their shop from about 1910 until the late 1920s, and besides custom-fitted riding garb they specialized in suits and other finery for men. Steve Ashby and Harry Triplett later worked with Shirley. His shop closed about 1940.

At the west end of town that jack-of-trades, Thomas Dunbar had his shop across from the Carr place; one building, I recall, yet remains. To the east, in front of an old graveyard, Charles Cleveland Kenny ran a store from the teens until the early 1930s, and across the street was Howard Staples' second blacksmith shop, which again in the thirties he shared with Charlie Wiltshire. In back of the shop was a wheelwright shop which had seen better days in an auto-less era. Mr. Kenny's store burned about 1957; the shops are long gone.

Fox hunting was nothing new to Upperville, but the bright garb and pomp and pageantry began in 1905, when on the porch of Dulin Laws' hotel, rules for the first English-U. S. foxhound match were written and signed by Henry A. Higginson of Great Britain and Harry Worcester Smith of Worcester, Massachusetts. They decreed the fox must be killed. It wasn't, but the American hounds were judged superior. It had been a dry fall, and the English hounds had been trained in their typically wet weather. Mr. Higginson was so irked at the outcome he pleaded "illness" and declined to attend the post-match festivities held at Welbourne. Judging from the Britisher's photograph, George Bernard Shaw might have used him for a model in *Pygmalion* and thus the Henry Higgins of *My Fair Lady.*

And one cannot forget the Upperville Library, the last of the Virginia Piedmont's subscription libraries. Ladies of the town organized the library in 1932, and May Calvert donated the building on her land, once the 1804-1845 office of first town physician Thomas W. Smith. Nora Dillard was the first librarian, followed by Ada Gibson Auty in 1932. She generally was there from 3-5 p.m. each Thursday (library hours) until her death in 1981. The library used to buy six books a month. Many books were, and continue to be, donated. Membership was $2 a year, up a dollar in 1981.

And so the Upperville image of the '20s through '50s, and a few years more: once a sleepy town with no traffic on Columbia Street, punctuated by blares from hunters' bugles in the frosty fall.

Paris

A Punkin' Turned Into A Coach

We are now fully in Fauquier County, but it would be remiss not to include this last pikeside village east of the Blue Ridge. Before 1957 one's vehicle had to pass through Paris before climbing the mountain.

Fauquier County was formed from Prince William County in 1758, and was named for Sir Francis Fauquier, Lieutenant Governor and Commander-in-Chief of armed forces in Virginia, 1758-68. As a talented economist, musician, and classicist, Sir Francis was made a Fellow of the Royal Society in 1753. Thomas Jefferson later called him "the ablest man who ever fulfilled the chair of government here."

The boundary between Loudoun and Fauquier—and across the Blue Ridge, Clarke County, carved from Frederick County in 1836—is marked by a stone, the date "1909," when the Fauquier-Clarke line was surveyed, and the number "20." Then, the marker stood by the skeleton of what was called "The Old Poplar." Before 1909, however, the same spot, termed "Poplar Corner" by surveyor George Love in 1824, was the westerly point of the newly surveyed Loudoun-Fauquier line.

The poplar in the cleft of Ashby's Gap first achieved some local status in 1844. During the presidential campaign, Whigs raised a Henry Clay and Theodore Frelinghuysen flag atop the poplar. After a few days the Democrats "crept up in the middle of the night," recalled area historian Curtis B. Chappelear, "and cut it [the flag] down." Underneath the tree many an officer camped during the Civil War, gazing out upon a Crooked Run valley that has changed little in 160 years. The poplar met its end some years later when zealous coon hunters burned the tree to smoke out their prey. Its skeleton stood until 1923, when U. S. Route 50 was paved and widened through the gap.

Early settler Thomas Ashby lived in the gap during the 18th century's first decades, and the 1,030-foot-high crevice in the Blue Ridge takes his name. Initially it was called an Indian Thoroughfare, and in colonial times Ashby's Bent—the latter word a Middle English word for hillside field.

We can thank the Piedmont Environmental Council for the sloping fields that yet mark the eastern approach to Ashby's Gap. Faced with a large-lot subdivision up these slopes—one house to 50 acres I recall—the PEC purchased 1,235 acres of Ovoka Farm in December of 1990. Only one better event ever happened to Paris, for we have a view described by traveler Andrew Burnaby in May 1759:

> When I got to the top, I was inexpressibly delighted with the scene which opened before me. Immediately under the mountain, which is covered with chamoedaphnes in full bloom, was a most beautiful scene: beyond this an extensive plain, diversified with every pleasing object that nature can exhibit.

Peter Glascock began the village in 1790, when he laid out lots on his 60 acres. As with all approaches to a mountain, especially one where two major roads–the Gap Road and Dumfries Road (now U. S. Route 17)–came together, the site cried for a stopover and blacksmith and wheelwright shop. Wagons needed adjusting before (or after) negotiating a height.

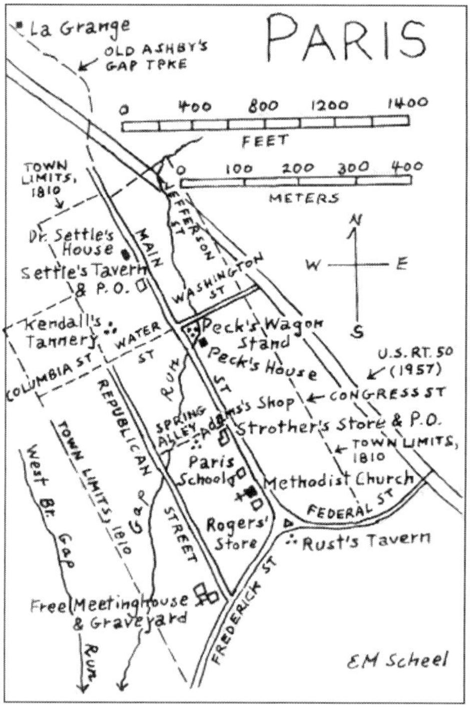

His village, which may have been little more than a huddle of houses, had no name other than "Punkin' Ville." And if you've read the Bluemont history in Volume Four, you may recall that Bluemont, its situation similar to that of Paris, was initially called "Punkin' Town." Those names had nothing to do with the oft-told stories of pumpkins rolling down the mountain after being spilt from an errant wagon. Rather, in Virginia-ese, the word "punkin" means an insignificant and out-of-way place. Remember the old hillbilly song, "Aaron Slick from Punkin' Crik"?

But in 1801 the village post office, second oldest post in Fauquier, is named Paris, and when the Virginia General Assembly charters the town in 1810, the new name still holds. Peter Glascock had fought in the American Revolution, and as an admirer of the Marquis de Lafayette, who had left the pleasures of France to fight for the American cause,

Mr. Glascock named his town for the French capital. Mr. Glascock also named his house, which overlooked Paris, LaGrange–the name of the Marquis' farm and a close-by village. Peter Glascock told the Marquis of his naming, and even offered him some lots in Paris. The Marquis graciously declined, but then said, "My dear sir, in order to hold you in memory, I shall, upon my return home, have a street in the town of LaGrange named Glascock."

By the 19th century's first decade, and possibly even before, Peter Rust had a tavern in the village. Thomson Ashby took over about 1820, and under various owners it remained a village stopover well after the Civil War. Of other businesses little is readily known, but Loudoun geographer Yardley Taylor gives some 200 Parisians high marks in 1835:

> This village enjoys a pure atmosphere, good water, and good health at all seasons; a disease of a local character has never been known to invade it–the people are intelligent and industrious; famed for their moral deportment and hospitality. The practice of gaming and horse racing, once the favorite amusements of the place and its vicinity, have now entirely gone out of vogue.

For some prominent village personalities, mentioned by old-timer Curtis Chappelear, we begin with John Hill, who about 1835 ended his many years of horsebacking the mail from Falmounth and Fredericksburg. From Isaac Settle's Tavern and post office, a fixture since about 1800, stagecoaches now plied the 60 miles to Washington. The fare was a steep $3.75–equivalent to what a limo ride to the capital would now cost. The fare to Winchester, 20 miles west, was $1.25. Other stages connected Paris with Alexandria and Fredericksburg. Most ran regularly until about 1852, when the Manassas Gap Railroad reached Delaplane.

One of the stage drivers was Andrew Longcord, a New Yorker who wore shoes with soles fastened with wooden pegs–unheard of south of the Potomac River. Mr. Longcord came to town as driver of a circus wagon, liked the situation, and as a shoemaker brought the concept of pegged shoes to town. He was also the village tailor for many years.

With its 200 or so people, Paris was big enough to warrant a yearly visit by the circus. Once a near-cyclone arose during the tent show. Spectators rushed for the exit but were blocked by a formidable showman who claimed there wasn't any danger. Captain Lewis Edmonds then stepped in, knocked the showman flat, and the crowd left. Good thing, too, for in a few minutes the tent blew in.

At six-foot-three and 250 pounds, Edmonds was the biggest man around, and surprisingly he was the best runner. Once at a state fair in Richmond, he took the measure of a former national champion. Every Fourth of July, Edmonds would again mop up the running races at the annual celebrations held at the east end of town. The village also held wrestling matches and by noon would start to roast an ox. The evening meal was free, a dance would end the day, and the politicians would all go home. Celebrations were the one event where townsmen and gentlemen farmers would mingle with the mountain people, cultivators of rocky soil and cutters of timber.

For two decades, beginning about 1812 when their house arose, William and Ann Peck had what was called a "wagoners' stand" at their home. The drivers could sleep inside, or stay outside with their four- and six-horse-team wagons, laden with goods from Alexandria or produce from the Shenandoah Valley. By the mid 1830s, when the railroad connected Winchester with Harper's Ferry, the wagoners took their produce to those towns. At the Ferry, rail and canal linked the Valley to the seaports of Alexandria and Baltimore. The Pecks' wagoner trade had seen its day.

Of some other remembered prewar villagers, Curtis Chappelear heard that three Parisians under the direction of Mechanicsville's (Scuffleburg today) Benjamin O'Rear, built the first horse-powered threshing machine to separate grain from straw and chaff. John Turner and Frank Ash built the treadmill and woodwork, and Orange Dougherty, the ironwork. That would have been about 1825.

Peter Hartman was one of the best-remembered craftsmen. He had walked from York, Pennsylvania, to Berryville about the same time, and at the center of town set his cane upright and told the curious that he would go in whatever direction the cane fell. Three times the cane fell on the road to Berry's Ferry, and there he walked. At the Shenandoah he came upon Joseph Glascock, son of the town founder, and on hearing Mr. Hartman' story, Mr. Glascock was so impressed that he told Hartman, the wanderer, to get on his horse and come with him to Paris. Mr. Glascock gave the tailor a rent-free room and a place to do business, and for 54 years Mr. Hartman was a Paris tailor.

Paris's most famous personality of both prewar and postwar years was Dr. Thomas L. Settle, grandson of Isaac Settle. His medical practice in Paris and surround spanned nearly sixty years. When war came he enlisted as a private, and as Major Settle he was surgeon for the 7th Virginia Cavalry. At the June 21, 1863, cavalry engagement at Upperville, Dr. Settle saved the life of Colonel Charles T. O'Ferrall. He had been left for dead on the field, but Alfred Ferguson, a passing soldier, spied some movement and called in the doctor. Colonel O'Ferrall recovered to become governor of Virginia.

Many years later, when, about 1910, foxhunters started to come into the area, Dr. Settle was called upon by a dowager who complained that her filly was a bit lackluster. One must add that physicians also served as veterinarians. The lady wondered if some saltpeter might help the filly's temperament. "Ma'am," Dr. Settle replied, "what that horse needs is real peter."

The best Civil War story Parisians recall took place at Berry's Ferry on the Shenandoah in April 1862. Union forces, under command of Brigadier General Louis Blenker had marched from Washington and were encamped at Paris. Next morning they marched down to the Shenandoah to cross, but rains had swollen the river. The Confederates had burned *Jeff Davis* the old ferry boat, but some of the "Dutchmen"–they were mostly German troops–found the boat and felt they could repair it. They did, and as they launched *Jeff Davis*, an old woman watching nearby said, "I hope *Jeff Davis* will sink and drown all of you." And in the hard midstream current the boat broke apart, drowning all aboard except a woman whose hoop skirt kept her afloat.

With the prime days of the stagecoach, wagon teams–and even the circus–over, Paris became just another Piedmont town after the war. Yet, still true to its mountainside location, it had more than its share of blacksmith and wheelwright shops and "hotels," according to gazetteers of the late 19th and early 20th centuries.

Of such enterprises in this era were the combined smith, wheelwright, and wagon-making shops of John Quincy Adams, James W. Chappelle, and Joseph E. Campbell. Each operated for more than two decades. A related concern was the saddlery and harness-making and leather-working shop of first, William Kendall, and then John Kendall. The Kendalls also had competition from another saddler, James M. Rice, and in the early twentieth from Harry Owens. The hotels were short-lived, and in post-1911 years were generally referred to by their true names, "boarding houses," one run by Miss Bessie Bell.

Three large general-mercantile stores graced the village from the 1870s through the first two decades of the 20th century. The largest was certainly that of Lewis Strother, who often was postmaster. In his store the post remained until 1957. Nearly as big were stores operated by Warren Rogers and family from circa 1885 to 1926, and by Abner H. Slack, who also had a hotel in the1880s and '90s. His "Paris Hotel" was the old Rust's tavern. James W. Slack was the village's jeweler, watchmaker, and silversmith.

And there was one person who could equal the longevity of Dr. Thomas Settle's three-decade career—Douglas Gibson, a cattle dealer. There were other physicians, however, and in one house two doctors, E. Ackley Moore and Albin Sydney Payne, practiced from the close of the Civil War until 1908.

What sets Paris off from other towns noted in this volume, is the survival rate of antebellum buildings. They're nearly all there, including the circa 1830 Free Meetinghouse, built on land donated by town founder Peter Glascock, and the village's public school, 1880-1912. The second school of 1893-1938 also survives, as does builder H. S. Hanes's 1892 Methodist Church.

Only Peter Rust's old tavern is no more, victim of a brakeless truck which careened down old Route 50 in 1940 and ran right into the frame structure. Norman Ashby's Texaco service station replaced the tavern, but it, like most of the then few village businesses, closed in the years following 1957, when Routes 17 and 50 were re-routed to skirt the village.

Then the feelings were mixed, for there were many kin to the businesses left. You got used to the truck traffic, and there weren't but a few early-morning cars driving to Washington. Now, everyone realizes it's the best thing that ever took place in Paris.

Dover

Hixons, A Champe, Rogers, And McCormicks

Three thousand six hundred air miles west and south of the White Cliffs is Dover, Virginia, named by the Hixson family for their home-place, Dover, England, county seat of Kent. The original Dover took its name back in the 4th century when Roman conquerors named the seaport for diving birds that looked like doves. The Romans called the birds *dofra* or *dovorra,* names soon to be given to the seaport. Our Dover, straddling Route 50 about midway between Aldie and Middleburg, got its start about 1785, when the Virginia Legislature decided to put tolls on the circa 1740 Belhaven Road—oldest major toll road in the U. S.

At this time, James Hixson and his wife, Sarah—of the Quaker Hixsons who came from Dover, England, via Bucks County, Pennsylvania and into the Waterford area of Loudoun some decades before—had settled by the turnpike, possibly living at a now burned (and removed) clapboard home just north of the pike. To the west of their home, standing today, rests a reported stone tollhouse with a massive chimney. If rumors are true, it's the only surviving tollhouse on the Ashby's Gap Turnpike and probably was erected about 1818 when the turnpike was completed.

A bit ahead of the Hixsons came Arthur Rogers and his wife, Mary McFall. Arthur was descended from a Scotch Presbyterian family who moved to County Antrim in the South of Ireland in the mid 16th century. One of Arthur's four children was Hugh Rogers, and one of Hugh's eleven children was William, who married the girl next door, Elizabeth Hixson, daughter of James.

In 1791, Sergeant John Champe returned to Loudoun from his unsuccessful attempt to capture traitor Benedict Arnold in December 1780. Champe was born close by on the ford road bearing his family name and rented a stone house a quarter-mile east of Dover. His adventures, detailed in C. A. Goodrich's *History of the United States* (1824), are romanticized in this period poem, author unknown. The Lee in the poem is Major Henry (Light Horse Harry) Lee; the general is George Washington.

Come, Sheathe your swords, my gallant boys,
And listen to the story,
How Sergeant Champe, one gloomy night,
Set off to catch the tory.

You see the General had got mad,
To think his plans were thwarted,
And swore by all, both good and bad,
That Arnold should be carted.

So unto Lee he sent a line,
And told him all his sorrow
And said that he must start the hunt,
Before the coming morrow.

Lee found a sergeant in his camp,
Made up of bone and muscle,
Who ne'er knew fear, and many a year
With tories had a tussle.

Bold Champe, when mounted on old Rip,
All buttoned up from weather,
Sang out good bye, cracked off his whip,
And soon was in the heather.

Another formidable house, west of Champe's place, was that of James and Sarah Hixson. They probably built the center stone wing of the three-section stone house, now Dover Farm, on a hill on the south side of the turnpike in 1790; the Hixsons added a larger west wing a decade or so later. The new wing's second story was of marble from the Goose Creek quarry. On a deed dated January 19, 1821, for $300 they sold to their son, Benjamin, three acres and a bit, just east of their homeplace, set inside "stone markers marked B. H. set on the south side of the turnpike." The steep price was undoubtedly due to the turnpike's completion.

PHOTO COURTESY THOMAS BALCH LIBRARY
The old quarters in 1976

PHOTO COURTESY THOMAS BALCH LIBRARY

James and Sarah Hixon's 1790 Dover house

Shortly after young Hixson bought the three acres, he had some accomplished laborers—probably under foreman William Benton, master builder of Oak Hill and the builder of his day in the Middleburg area—build a two-wing Federal style brick house. Its front is of fine Flemish bond, the practice of laying brick by alternating headers and stretchers in each row. This house, called Dover, was most likely built in expectation of Ben's marriage to Tacey Humphrey.

Before building, Ben Hixson may have lived in the cottage his parents once occupied, soon to be a shop for manufacturing nails. Just across the pike from the shop, also standing today, a shingled and stone cottage was built to house the Hixson servants or the miller-to-be of a three story stone affair that was going up next door. The manufactory was called Dover Mills. The plural usage derives from the mill's three grinding stones (or burrs), each a mill in itself, grinding a different grain. While there was sadness in the home of Ben and Tacey Hixson because of the loss of three young children, the mill, nail shop, and Hixson holdings of hundreds of acres prospered.

But, the Hixson holdings did not appear to recover after the financial crises of 1837 and 1840. On May 28, 1846, they sold 183 acres to their surviving son, John, for $4,579, and in 1850, they sold 74 acres for $3,000 to William Rogers; the latter tract included the stone Hixson homeplace. Two years later the Hixsons owed debts totaling $3,230, and they were forced to sell the brick house called Dover. In 1852 the land was granted to neighbor, relative by marriage, and friend, William Rogers, so that Rogers could auction off "the tract of Land on which the said Hixson now resides, including the Mill property known as Dover Mills." Mrs. Hixson was in ill health, and that January her three-year-old grandson, Joseph Reid, died. Rogers mercifully postponed the auction until she died. It was one of many kind acts that earned Mr. Rogers the nickname "Extra Billy." Rogers sold the homeplace late in 1854, and its deed, recorded the first day of the new year, notes: "The said Robert B. McCormick, being the highest bidder, became the purchaser of the dwelling house and lot in Dover: the late residence of said Benjamin Hixson." The selling price was $5,000, so the debts were paid.

Robert Burns McCormick came to Dover from Auburn in Fauquier County. Accompanying him was his bride, Katherine A. Reynolds of Clarke County. McCormick was kinsman to the inventor, Auburn's Stephen McCormick. The McCormick Plow, a cast-iron plow with detachable parts that plowed deeper and used fewer parts, revolutionized agriculture in the Virginia Piedmont in the 1830s and 1840s.

At Dover the McCormicks soon established an English and classical school, popularly known as Dover Academy. It was a co-ed school, though primarily for boys, with dormitories in the three-dormered attic. The McCormicks stressed discipline and taught the three Rs, and Greek, Latin, French, astronomy, and higher mathematics. Dover Academy was one of the few area private schools to survive the Civil War. It closed in 1888.

Besides teaching, Katherine McCormick kept busy. Here is her weekly schedule:

> Monday: Clean upstairs rooms and basement steps and landing
> Tuesday: Wash own clothes and bathroom floors
> Wed: Clean windows glass door in office & iron clothes
> Thurs: Clean white woodwork & bathroom floors
> Friday: Clean silver or brasses
> Sat: Clean bathroom floors wash steps & hall & round [turn over] the rugs in dining room & office

The McCormicks were not slaveholders and early in the war were suspected Northern sympathizers. Since Dover was a strategic pass-through for the armies, Robert was jailed in Alexandria. He was not there long and came back in March or April 1862, to see his home occupied by Union Brigadier General Jacob Bowman Sweitzer's brigade of the Army of the Potomac. Robert McCormick and Jacob Sweitzer became close friends, and when Mr. McCormick' son, Charles, later went to the Naval Academy, he roomed with Midshipman Joseph Strauss, who married General Sweitzer's only daughter.

Two war babies of the McCormicks achieved fame. Charles Monard McCormick, a Naval Academy graduate, prepared the first nautical chart of the Easter Island in 1887, and brought several of the islands' stone monoliths to the National Museum (today's Smithsonian), where their plaques bear his name. In May 1898 he commanded the gun crew that fired the first shot at Manila Bay, and later sank the *Regina Cristina,* flagship of the seven-vessel Spanish squadron. Willoughby Monard McCormick, in 1889 founded and became president of McCormick & Company, Baltimore, that spice-and-tea House of McCormick.

At Oakham House, a little more than a half-mile west of Dover, Colonel J. E. B. Stuart had his headquarters late in 1862. That December, a Southwest Virginia lawyer by the name of John Singleton Mosby, a lieutenant in Stuart's command, began his famous career as the *beau sabreur*, the dashing centaur of "The Debatable Land of Loudoun and Fauquier." To quote Mosby's *War Reminiscences* of 1887:

> Having learned by the telegraph that Fairfax Court House was held by a brigade of infantry, Stuart marched around north of it, and went into Loudoun–a land flowing with plenty. He made his headquarters at Colonel [Hamilton] Rogers', near Dover, and rested until the next day. On the morning he left, I went into his room, and asked him to let me stay behind for a few days with a squad of men. I thought I could do something with them. He readily asserted. I got nine men–including, of course, Beattie–who volunteered to go with me. This was the beginning of my career as a partisan.

In November 1864, Thomas Watson, the last miller at Dover Mills, ripped out the millworks so Federal Major General Wesley Merritt's troops wouldn't have the satisfaction of destroying the mill during their burning raids through western Loudoun. At this time Dover House was used as a hospital for wounded Confederate soldiers, and it has been said that the patients "slept all day and rode all night."

Charles McCormick, along with Claude Saffer and others, financed the first paving of a road in Loudoun County in the summers of 1913 and 1914. The new seven-mile toll road went from Mount Zion Church, past Dover, to Middleburg. In 1924, Charles McCormick gave stones from the walls of the redundant Dover Mills to the Middleburg National Bank. Willie Hall and his crew dismantled the mill in one day, and one startled motorist, his familiar landmark missing, drove right into the mill race. Hall and crew then built the town's first bank, at the southeast corner of Washington and Madison, with Dover Mills stone. Mr. McCormick also donated one of the millstones to the bank, and it is there today. The remaining two stayed, flanking the Dover walkway.

Dover received its post office in 1877, and as expected, Robert Burns McCormick was the first postmaster. The post office was always at Dover House, just left of the main entrance. Daughter Harriett "Hattie" McCormick closed its doors in 1904, when RFD sent the mails back to Middleburg.

John Champe's house, PHOTO COURTESY THOMAS BALCH LIBRARY

In 1940 the State Highway Department took out the sharp curve at Dover and put in present Route 50 just to the south. To save Dover Spring, once inside the mill, and supplier of water for every village home beside the brick Hixson house, they enclosed the spring in concrete and put in four steps leading to it. Just north of the spring you can still see the remains of Dover Mills' walls–stone the bank didn't need.

Just west of the spring, the road sign, "Cobb House Road," is the successor to one of several road markers put up by the Aldie Horticultural Society in 1963, the first rural road signs in Loudoun County. The signs were dedicated to Alice C. Hutchison, who remembered the names she had heard as a girl. Old timers told me the log house used to be a rendezvous point for Mosby's men, and later a Cobb family lived there.

The building, at the Snickersville Pike corner, came down about 1940.

The walls of John Champe's stone house, lived in by Sergeant Champe for about fifteen years, crumbled around 1915, and the spring across the road, known as Champe's Spring, dried up some years before. The state put up a marker honoring Sergeant Champe in 1928. An 11-foot-high obelisk was erected at the house site in 1941 with stone from the home's ruins. On a bronze plaque is the wording "Here Was the Home of Sergeant John Champe Continental Army Who Risked the Inglorious Death of a Spy for the Independence of His Country."

Colonel Floyd W. Harris of nearby Stoke was responsible for the stone marker. He became intrigued with Champe's exploits after reading a detailed account in *Blackwood's Magazine* of how a Captain Cameron of Benedict Arnold's old command was traveling with a servant in Loudoun County and was overtaken by night and a thunderstorm. The wayfarers sought shelter, cordially provided by the man of the house. But, as the table was prepared and the coals in the fire stirred for warmth, in the glimmering light Captain Cameron recognized John Champe, the man he had enlisted in the British army a half-decade before. The entire tale is worthy of grand opera.

Atoka

Where Stuart Miscalculated And Mosby Wept

When Grover Cleveland campaigned for his first Presidency in 1884, one of his kept promises was "a post office every four miles" so people wouldn't have to walk more than two miles one way. Within a few years the country had hundreds of new post offices, and to assist locals who couldn't think of a name, the Post Office Department had a list of three-to-five-word easy-to-spell names; Atoka was on that list.

There had been a village on the spot since October 1838 when Elijah M. Anderson became first postmaster of "Rector's X Roads," as it appears on U. S. postal ledgers. The post office had been named for the Rector family, with a possible nod to Henry Rector of present Rectortown, who in 1764 received one of the last area grants, 237 acres "on the drains of Goose Creek."

PHOTO COURTESY THOMAS BALCH LIBRARY

The 1819 Lemmon's Bottom Bridge carried traffic over Goose Creek until 1957

Beside the crossroads there was a fine spring on the tableland and the area had been a favorite spot for temperance picnics, jousting tournaments, and religious camp meetings. Less than a mile to the west, the magnificent four-arch, seven-buttress stone bridge, completed in 1819, spanned Goose Creek, and in spring, 1820, the Virginia General Assembly authorized the Ashby's Gap Turnpike Company to erect a toll-house to provide funds "for the use of said bridge, and for the fractional part of a section of the turnpike road."

The oldest store in memory is that of David B. Denham, built in 1851 at the site of the present store. But there may have been a store there during Elijah Anderson's time, and the years of Joseph A. Taylor, who followed Anderson as postmaster in 1845, and served until 1853. For reasons unknown, the post office closed in December of that year and did not reopen until war clouds were brewing in April 1860. John Martz was now postmaster, and he served under the Confederate administration–the reason for his being fired in June 1865, and for the closing of the post office. Two year later the U. S. government forgave Mr. Martz, and the Rector's X Roads post office lingered until 1868.

PHOTO COURTESY *MOSBY'S CONFEDERACY*

By Lakeland School Mosby first met his command

On the Atoka Road, seven-tenths of a mile south of the village, sits the refurbished stuccoed Lakeland School, the one surviving prewar public building. A predecessor of this school, possibly at the same location, dated from about 1795, and was built to educate the children of Isaac and James Lake. Their stone house, Lakeland, built by and for Loudoun stonemason Daniel Morin in 1787, stands in fine condition west of the school by the old roadbed. The present school dates from the 1840s, and was also built to educate Lake children. It is one of the area's few surviving field schools or old-field schools, so-called because farmers allowed them to be constructed at the edges of their old fields—fields once cultivated but lying fallow. About 1885 this school became a public school, with the name Atoka. It closed about 1915.

Civil War events and troop movements were commonplace to the village, especially during the westward push by Union forces along the Ashby's Gap Turnpike, June 17-21, 1863. But it was an event earlier that month that brings pilgrims, for John Singleton Mosby organized his 43rd Battalion Partisan Rangers at Atoka.

Less than six months before, at Oakham, some six miles east on the same turnpike, Lieutenant Mosby had received permission from J. E. B. Stuart, his commanding officer, to go and maraud with nine men.

As Oakham and its grounds retain the appearance of antebellum years, so do the sites at Rector's Crossroads. The stuccoed-stone house of Clinton Caleb Rector, where Mosby met with his four officers-to-be; the stone springhouse where they repaired for water that hot June 10; and the woods by Lakeland School, where Mosby and the officers met with the men that would become Co. A of the 43rd Battalion, remain much as they were in 1863. While records do not survive noting the initial members of Co. A (reportedly the rosters were destroyed when Federal troops burned Heartland, the Joseph Blackwell place, deep into upper Fauquier, in 1864), old-timers say there were some two-dozen who tethered their horses in the schoolhouse woods.

Mosby had already developed the secret of his success by June, noted in his 1887 *War Reminiscences*. "I often sent small squads at night to attack and run in the pickets along a line of several miles. Of course, these alarms were very annoying, for no human being knows how sweet sleep is but a soldier."

A 1994 letter of Annie Rector's granddaughter, Dorothy Rector adds some tinsel to Mosbyana. Regarding the famed June 10 meeting:

> "the documents were signed in the living room or parlor as my Grandma Rector recalled. She also spoke often of the visit she had with Colonel Mosby. He came to the house after the war and asked to see the room where he formed the Rangers. Grandma said he entered the room—then sat down and wept."

Before the 1863 Battle of Gettysburg, General J. E. B. Stuart and troops camped by the Rector place on a rainy June 23. As was his custom, the general slept outdoors with his men. But he told his aide, Major Henry B. McClellan, to sleep on the porch, for he was to receive a communiqué from General Robert E. Lee. This order would inform General Stuart that he was to proceed northward by crossing the lower Potomac River fords. Jeb Stuart did just that, choosing Rowzie's (usually called Rowser's) at Lowe's Island in lower Loudoun. As the ford was deep because of heavy rains, Stuart's cavalry, 4,000 strong, could not cross easily and arrived late on the Battle of Gettysburg's second day. And as General Lee's communiqué was lost in the campaign, Civil War buffs constantly debate the wisdom of Stuart's movements. If he had arrived at Gettysburg before the battle began, would the outcome have been different? General Stuart didn't have time to comment about his detour, because he was killed at Yellow Tavern the following May.

These events have taken on new meaning since the summer of

1999, when the John Singleton Mosby Heritage Area organization bought the Rector place and moved there. The old house and grounds are open to visitors.

PHOTO COURTESY ATOKA PRESERVATION SOCIETY

The Clinton Rector place, where Mosby organized his Raiders

Rector's Crossroads slumbered until 1892, when Clarence Rector had the present store built. President Cleveland's promise of a post office every four miles was being carried through, and Zachary Pierce, who lived at Greenway (recently Senator John Warner's Atoka Farm), led the area movement to have a post office placed at Rector's Store.

When U. S. postal authorities came to the crossroads, they stayed at Greenway, and Mr. Pierce told them area residents preferred the old name, Rector's Crossroads. But the authorities said another name would have to be found because of the confusion with Rectortown, five miles to the south. Mr. Pierce couldn't think of another name, and so as was the custom, the authorities produced a list of names, most of them, for spellings' sakes from three to five letters. They told Mr. Pierce and locals that they could pick any name they wanted as long as it was not duplicated in Virginia or Vermont or Pennsylvania, for the latter two states' abbreviations could be confused with Virginia's. According to Mrs. Russell (Annie) Gregg, Zachary Pierce's daughter, "We finally chose Atoka because there was only one post office with that name and it was in Indian Territory [Oklahoma]." On July 3, 1893, U. S. Postmaster General John Wanamaker appointed Clyde W. Rector postmaster of Atoka, and he remained in that position until January 15, 1907, when Rural Free Delivery closed the office and the mails were brought by wagon from Middleburg.

Sometime between those years, probably before 1900, the old road into Atoka from the north was abandoned in favor of New Ford Road, a half-mile east of the village. The crossroads became a corner, though the name "Rector's X Roads," in parenthesis to Atoka, was retained on the 1914 Map of Fauquier County. The old road north can still be seen just west of the store.

PHOTO COURTESY THOMAS BALCH LIBRARY

Morris and Thelma Rector's store, about 1975

By 1924, Morris B. Rector was running the store, having taken over the job from Clarence Rector. Morris's wife, Thelma helped him, and in 1927, they added their drive-in porticoed gas station. The couple ran Rector's General Merchandise until Morris had a stroke in the late 1970s. In April 1977, the Rector family leased the store to Samuel and Barbara Jane Deane, and other operators have followed in their stead.

Nostalgia pervaded the village on July 15, 1933, the Centennial of John Mosby's birth, (actually December 6, 1833, but December was not the month for gatherings). Two chapters of the United Daughters of the Confederacy arranged the affairs at Oden Lake's Lakeland, where the severely wounded Mosby feigned death before an inebriated Union officer and then was whisked to safety. Boxwood's General Billy Mitchell opened with appropriate words, followed by Mr. Lake, Virginia Senator John Rust, and one surviving Confederate, General Magnus Thompson. The *Fauquier Democrat* noted, "nearly every one was a descendant or relative of one of Mosby's men." The state historical marker was set by the Clinton Rector place where Mosby first met with his command's officers (the marker was moved to its present Route 50 location in 1958). An aged Negro, a slave before the war, was introduced to polite applause. The hat was passed, with proceeds going toward restoring the gardens at Stratford Hall, birthplace of Robert E. Lee.

As a name, Atoka has always had the right ring, and more than a few newspapers and magazines carried the dateline "Atoka, Va." when it was announced that President and Mrs. John F. Kennedy bought 39 acres a mile southeast of the village for $26,000 in 1962. On this 582-foot-high hill, locally known as Hatcher's Hill, the Kennedys built their concrete-block rambler. They named the house Wexford, for the President's home county in Ireland. The house remains a private residence today.

Fauquier historian Harry C. Groome noted Atoka's population as 20 in 1914, and because of smaller families, it's down to about 15 today. But you can easily get together a quorum of five adults by stepping inside Rector's store—capital of Atoka since the days of the Indian Territory.

Pot House

A Surge Of Leiths Followed The Bentons' Demise

First mention of a Pot House in Loudoun came in 1796, when the Reverend Alexander McFarland, rector of Cameron Parish, wrote that he preached at the "Pot-House" once a month. And in May of that year his words were clarified by an advertisement in the *Alexandria Gazette*, placed by Joseph Lane of nearby Farmer's Delight

> "will sell or let a COMPLETE POT HOUSE The Pot House includes the Kiln. House is about 60 feet in length and 20 feet in breadth. It is two story high, and has room laid off, with fireplace, etc. for the accommodation of a family. Every necessary and convenience for the Potter's Business are already on the premises. The situation will be found inviting: and the great demand for Earthen Ware and the rapid consumption encouraging."

At a later date, the purchaser was William Benton, who had come to Loudoun from the English village of Lisbon, Lincolnshire, in the early 1800s. During the War of 1812, Mr. Benton, then a soldier, came to know Secretary of State James Monroe. According to the family, Mr. Benton then became the future president's "[farm] overseer, steward, counselor, and friend." When President Monroe was planning Oak Hill in 1820, he commended Mr. Benton's brick-making and brick-laying abilities to William Hoban, architect of Oak Hill. Mr. Benton got the job, and his craftsmanship and bricks from his Pot House kiln not only graced Oak Hill, but a score of other notable structures of ante-bellum Loudoun: Woodburn, the "brick house" at Foxcroft, the Unison Methodist Church, Middleburg Free Church, Emannuel Church parsonage, and Spring Hill (later Benton), his home.

Mr. Benton might have returned to England after the War of 1812 because his wife, Sarah Hyde, through inheritance, had a claim on Hyde Park. But the king was confiscating right and left, and the Empire's loss was Loudoun's gain. With the moneys he received for building Oak Hill, he bought 300 acres from John and Sarah Martin for $20 on October 24, 1821. The site was by the Pot House crossroads, where the kiln fired the family income. William Benton lived until age 99. He was breaking a colt, which ran under a tree limb and knocked Mr. Benton off. He died of complications and pneumonia.

William Benton's son was born, September 19, 1819, at one of the older houses on Oak Hill grounds. He was christened James Monroe Benton, 2nd. His godparents were President and Mrs. Monroe. In 1837, the younger Benton followed his father's stead, and helped him build New Lisbon, a new Benton home close to the Pot House.

During the 1840s there was a school at New Lisbon, run by Benjamin Hyde Benton and called the Lisbon Institute. In his advertisement "for scholars" in the October 11, 1845 *Warrenton Times*, he noted a reduced board of $68 and a tuition of $12 to $32 for a 10-month term rather reasonable rates. Courses of study included a workshop in metals, Latin, Greek, analytical and spherical trigonometry, and surveying. Among the institute's "extensive" equipment were maps, globes, and "chemical and philosophical apparatus."

By 1851 Benjamin Hyde Benton had left New Lisbon to found the Loudoun Agricultural and Chemical Institute north of Aldie, and William B. Carr became principal of the mother school, now the New Lisbon Institute. His term that year began January 6th, ran twenty-six weeks, and his *Washingtonian* ad assured parents the "situation eminently healthy" and the neighborhood "moral and intelligent. Being in the country, the student is of course, free from the allurements to vice and dissipation, to which he is exposed in city or town." New Lisbon Institute closed in 1853, but professor Carr taught on, and in 1885 was president of Leesburg Academy.

A New Lisbon Female Academy advertised in *The Washingtonian* in January 1854, with Mrs. E. H. Green "Principal preceptress" and Helen S. Benedict "Teacher of French, Music on Piano and Organ, Dancing and Painting." We hear no more of the venture, but that is not the end of prewar schooling at New Lisbon. In defiance of state law, Benjamin Benton taught his slaves (he owned 19 in 1850) to read and write.

Knowing that he would enlist in the Confederate services, James Monroe Benton leased New Lisbon for five years to Dr. J. A. Hayes, a Baptist preacher from Middleburg. During the war years the farm again became a girl's school. Hearing that the Yankees were to burn the home—Benton being a rather gung-ho officer with General Beauregard—Mrs. Benton, the former Margaret Harrison, with the help of the servants, moved out during the night. She and the children went to Aspen Hill, Benton's winter home, between Fairfax Court House and Alexandria. When they left Aspen Hill, they left behind a collection of rare china and crockery, hidden in the floorboards. The Federals found the collection, broke it with their swords, and burned Aspen Hill.

After Lincoln's Emancipation Proclamation of September 22, 1863, none of the slaves at New Lisbon left the plantation. As ex-slaves they stayed on, and the Bentons gave some of them land.

Times were difficult though, and the family remembers how they used three-inch-long thorns for hairpins and chickory weed in place of coffee. James Monroe Benton had invested heavily in Confederate bonds and dollars, and with the war ended and their livestock driven off, they nor the family had little else. He died in 1875, and in 1900 his heirs sold New Lisbon's 413 acres to Annie Leith for $8,000.

During the U. S. Bicentennial Year, William T. Leith, owner of Benton, wrote a history of his family and of the village that would take their name. The Leiths took their name from the town of Leith, a seaport for Edinburgh, Scotland, and the first Leith of record was William, Provost of Aberdeen, in 1350. Almost 400 years later, "Jamie the Scot," as the patriarchal Leiths called him, migrated to Loudoun County, then part of Fairfax.

On September 9, 1768, James Leith for £240, bought 620 acres on Goose Creek "where Hugh McCaffrey now lives." Today that land comprises the old Frederick Warburgs' Snake Hill Farm, and on it lies a burial ground where James Leith was interred about 1800.

One of Jamie's grandsons, William G. Leith, spawned what was later known as the "Leithton crowd." He had a daughter and five sons. One son, Benjamin Franklin Leith, settled on the old Hugh McCaffrey place. Randolph Howard Leith married Martha Gregg, great-granddaughter of Colonel James Lane, who had seen to the building of Farmer's Delight from 1770-1783.

The other three sons, Theodoric B., James, usually called Tim, and Lawrence, went to war, riding with Mosby and Stuart. After the stillness at Appomattox they returned home to the brick house at Snake Hill, where their father was living. Tim married his cousin Frances Leith, and they raised their family at today's Foxcroft. Theo married Anna Gregg. They raised their family at Turkey Roost. She was the "Mrs. Annie Leith" mentioned in the 1900 New Lisbon Deed. Lawrence married Louisa Osborn and lived at Locust Shade, said to have been one of the loveliest of Leith homes.

Will Leith, who had known them all when young, called his forebears "musical, worldly, sometimes a bit wild, but always pleasant to have around. High life, wine, horses, and song scattered the family somewhat, but they all enjoyed the good life in Loudoun County."

Howard and Martha Leith sold to Mercer District School Trustees, land for the first Pot House School. The date was February 3, 1875. The price was $37.50 for three-eighths of an acre "on which there is a new School House." Teachers at the school were Lottie Chamblin, Nettie Gibson, Frank Tyler, and Dr. Billy Gregg, Martha Leith's brother. He had a well remembered "dictionary class." If you spelled a word correctly and gave the meaning of it, you sat at the head of the class.

The post was in William Benton's brick house on the northeast corner. Theodoric S. Manuel was postmaster in 1894 opening the office that May 21. William G. Leith followed in 1896, and John W. Symons in 1898. Symons ran the post and store for a few years, and then John W. Ignatius closed its doors November 17, 1904. The RFD wagon now made its daily run from Middleburg. There was a store at the brick house as early as 1870, and in the last decades of the 19th century, Harry Anderson, John Carpenter, and Joseph and Theodoric Manuel ran it. A July 20, 1894 "Leithton Letter," datelined "Leithton (formerly Pot House)" offered some insights. "Since the boom has struck our little village and it has assumed a more euphonious name, we think it deserving of some note." *The Hamilton Telephone*'s writer goes on to tell that William Seaton ran a wheelwright shop, Joseph Reed a blacksmith shop, and Joseph Manuel was postmaster.

Stephen Monroe Benton, one of William Benton's sons, ran the blacksmith shop at Pot House in the 1880s, and he was followed by Joseph Reed, then by Frank "Nub" Reed Jr., about 1900. A decade later Jesse Bell became the smith, and then came Eugene Downs, who also ran the store in the late teens. Eugene's brother, Erman Downs, was smith for three years. He left in 1915. In these later years, the store shifted across the road next to the still-standing blacksmith shop. A familiar crowd in front of the blacksmith shop in the 1890s and early 1900s were the five old Leith brothers, who would sit by its overhang, tell war stories, and chew Arthur Leith's homegrown tobacco.

By 1917 Foxcroft School owned the brick house, and Miss Charlotte had it painted pink. And at the pink house, as everyone now calls the dwelling, in October 1935, Loudoun's first free health-service program began, courtesy of Miss Charlotte. Lee McDonald was the nurse, and besides fixing the usual aches and pains, she forwarded such radical ideas as improved living conditions and free hospitalization. Those were the Roosevelt years; they even reached Pot House.

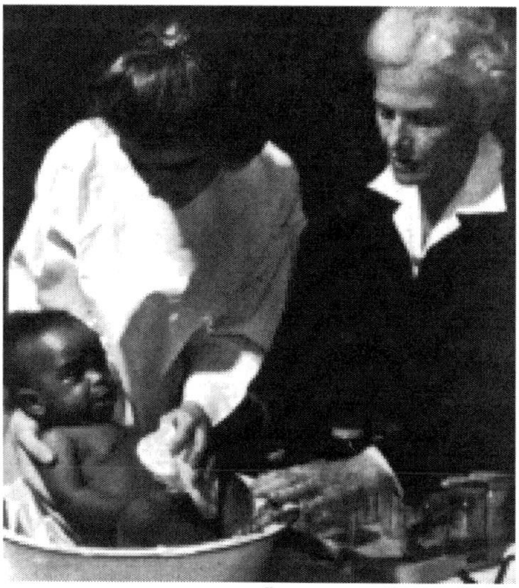

PHOTO COURTESY FOXCROFT SCHOOL

Loudoun's first free health clinic

A succession of keepers catered to sweet tooths of Foxcroft girls through the 1920s. After the Leithton store closed, Foxcroft girls would ride or walk two miles to Will Bolen's at Mountville for their bottle of pop. Thus, Charlotte Noland, Foxcroft headmistress, wanted to keep the road dirt. But at Mountville, Carl Furr wanted progress. Who won? See the Mountville history.

Miss Noland also had classic battles with latter-day Pot House schoolteachers. One who gave her a dilly was Olive Story from Chinquapin Neck country in Culpeper. Miss Story felt Miss Charlotte was something of a prig. Miss Charlotte sometimes looked askance at the public schools. She was quite happy, when in 1921, the public school moved from "her" side of the Pot House crossroads to across the road. She wasn't directly responsible for the move, though. It was a man by the name of Gordon Massey. He didn't want a school building in front of his lane, so he gave some money to Joseph L. and Arthur F. Leith and had them donate land for the second Pot House School, a two roomer that opened in 1921 and closed in 1984. The building still stands, as does most of old Pot House.

Charles S. Monroe, for whom Leesburg's Monroe Vocational Technical Center was named, was the last teacher at the old Pot House School, then officially called Leithton School. Enrollment was heavy, and he needed a staff. He hired Lina (Mrs. Edgar) Robey who taught the younger children at the brick house at Pot House Crossroads.

Mountville

Ezekial's Orchard Turned The Road

Mountville, or "Mountsville," as sloppy pronouncers have been known to call the village, was named for farmer Ezekial Mount, from Mountville, Pennsylvania. He came to Loudoun in 1796 and that June 11 bought 236 acres, described only as on "Goose Creek," from Henry and Mary Gulik, who were then living in Hunterdon County, New Jersey. The selling price was £200 (about $700). The land was then known as the old Cuthbert Harrison place.

In 1798 and 1809 Ezekial Mount added to his holdings by purchasing 14 acres and later another 75 acres from Burr and Catherine Powell. Both tracts, bought for £10 and £302, had once belonged to Thomas Chinn.

One incident insured the Mount name permanently. When the old Mountain or Middle Road, later the Snickers' Gap Turnpike, was put through from Aldie to Snickers' Gap, the road was almost a straight line, and that line ran right between Ezekial's stone barn and blacksmith shop. Too often horses being shod shied away from passing wagons and riders, and the threat of thievery bothered Ezekial. He began to wish the road were never there.

So he went to the courthouse and to the turnpike directors and asked them to shift the pike. They would not. Next he consulted a lawyer to see if anything could be done to remedy the situation. The lawyer had an idea. There was a law on Virginia books that said no road could be put through an orchard without the owner's permission.

Ezekial didn't have an orchard, but overnight he constructed one. His lawyer told him that an orchard was legally defined as one or more trees used for commercial purposes. So he had his slaves dig up an old apple tree, roots and all, and transplant it right in the middle of the turnpike between his barn and blacksmith shop. Of course he picked the month of October for transplanting, and the next day his slaves were picking apples off the tree and carting them to Middleburg. Ezekial's one-tree orchard moved the turnpike, so as you're negotiating that right-angle turn four miles north of Aldie on the Snickersville Pike, tip your hat to Ezekial Mount. Of course, Ezekial was so pleased with the outcome that he planted a whole orchard by the first tree. That all happened in 1814.

Ezekial was a good friend of neighbor William Benton from New Lisbon, as Pot House village was then called. One fall day in the 1820s, Mr. Mount mentioned to Mr. Benton that he couldn't get enough help to harvest his wheat. William thought he'd surprise Ezekial. It was a moonlit night, and Willliam had his many slaves cradle and shock the wheat that night. The next day when Ezekial looked out the window, there was the wheat, all neatly shocked.

Ezekial Mount died in 1834, and besides his land, left a sizeable estate of more that $5,000. To his family members, Mary, James, Thomas, and Stephen, he gave about $695. He had three sons, Charles, James and John—known as "Doc" or Doctor Mount, the area's first physician.

PHOTO COURTESY ROBERT L. HUMPHREY JR.

The Mount place, Creek Hill, circa 1890

When a post office was established at the corner of the pike and the road to New Lisbon, there was no question as to whose name it would carry. The year was 1817, the day January 27, and the name was spelled "Mountsville"—corrected eight years later. Ezekial's doctor son

John Mount was the first postmaster, followed in 1819 by Daniel Brown, and in 1826 by miller John Francis. Dr. Mount again took over in 1840, and Nancy Lumm, an early county postmistress, followed in 1854. Her husband John often helped her, and the Lumms held the office at least through 1866.

In 1835 local geographer Yardley Taylor described Mountville: "several dwelling houses, 1 mercantile store, 2 taverns, 1 manufacturing flour mill, 2 smith shops, 2 boot and shoe factories, and various other mechanics. Population 74." He also devoted some space to its land, "remarkably good, and is valued in market at 35 and 40 dollars an acre." And to the two Snickersville Pike bridges, by which one entered the neighborhood: "a superior wooden arched bridge" across Goose Creek and "and excellent one arch stone bridge" over Beaver Dam. This latter bridge was Hibbs' span.

At mid century the post office was usually in the main mercantile store of Elimelech Carter and William H. Francis, also the miller at the family's manufactory a mile south of the village on Goose Creek. The Mounts still owned the blacksmith shop, run by their slaves. The turnpike's tollhouse was initially a mile southeast of the village by George Washington McCarty's grist mill at the "superior" Carter's Bridge across Goose Creek, but sometime later it was moved to the village.

In summary, Mountville was the largest of the villages in that rich farm country between Middleburg and Philomont.

A church was long overdue, and in May 1852, John R. and Maria Carter donated an acre to the Methodist Episcopal Church South, a half-mile southwest of the village on the "road leading from New Lisbon to Mountsville." With Carter money and slaves the plastered stone Mountville Church was built that year. The church trustees read as a local who's who: John A. Beavers, William B. Carr, B. Franklin Carter, Francis M. Carter, Thomas Francis, William H. Francis, Stephen McCarty, and John E. and Charles E. Mount.

Mountsville—even the census taker added the 's'—had thirty-three people in 1870, and a post office reestablished December 21, 1868, under postmaster E. F. Hibbs, who might have run a store. In 1881, James M. Mount took over the postmaster's duties, for he and his brother, physician John E. Mount, had just opened a store, described as doing a great business in 1884. Across the road, William T. E. Bolen, who did not get along with the Mounts, opened a competing store in

1905, and Elisha H. Van Sickler had his post office there the same year. Opposite the village tollhouse, Will's father, Joseph Bolen, had his blacksmith shop.

During the late 19th century Gritland Mills and quarry on Goose Creek, once owned by the Francises was the leading area enterprise, and in 1884 was spoken of in glowing terms. "The whetstone quarries of Gritland are inexhaustible and of quality second to none in America." Farmer and miller George Z. Dodd and partner J. T. Megeath ran the manufactory in the 1870s and early 1880s; then John Ed Francis took over. His son, Edward Francis, ran an adjacent sawmill. Gritland Mills fell in during the May 1889 "Johnstown Flood." The partially reliable *Virginia Gazetteer* of J. H. Chataigne listed five millwrights in the county in 1885. Four were named Trenary, with two, James Trenary and John L. Trenary, at Mountville.

The village also had its private school, V. M. Johnson's coeducational "Mountville Academy," which opened its doors in September of 1874. Mr. Johnson and his wife, who taught music, had had a school

Photo courtesy Thomas Balch Library

Jim Mount's store, circa 1910

in Hamilton for two years, and he had previously taught at VMI. Its superintendent recommended Johnson highly, as did former Governor John Letcher and former Lieutenant Governor John L. Marye. No one recalls the school, and apparently it had long vanished when, in May 1887, the Mercer District School Board purchased an acre next to the

Mountville Church and proceeded to build the Mountville School, remembered for such teachers as Will Shackelford, Helen Gibson, Fenton Furr, Mabel Francis, and Mrs. John Ed Francis.

Mountville became the domain of William Thomas Edward Bolen, who had become storekeeper in 1905, and village postmaster in October, 1909. His position was strengthened when the old Mount store across the road closed about 1920. Will Bolen's sister, Kate Bolen, and his daughters, Helen and Dorothy, helped run the enterprise. In the late thirties he coaxed Jack Hibbs out of retirement, and he opened a butcher shop that lasted about a decade. The Mountville Post Office remained open until May 4th 1954, when Bolen retired, and the store closed about a year later. Joseph Bolen's blacksmith shop lingered on through the late 1930s. Of the family mill operated by Edward Francis, it was the last of the Goose Creek water mills to close, in the late 1920s.

Mountville Methodist Church, for eighty years the spiritual home of the Carters, Francises, McCartys, and Mounts, closed for lack of a congregation in the mid 1930s. The adjacent two-room stone school, a replacement for the frame one-roomer, was built by Charles Rhodes in 1931. It stayed open through the late forties. Curtis Hawes built a still standing bungalow from the old school's lumber.

The tollhouse, which closed in 1890, when tolls came off the Snickersville Pike, held a special place in the hearts of the Mount family–harking back to Ezekial's victory over the turnpike. In Dr. John Mount's will, he specifically gave the "toll-house and lot"–even though it was a tiny vacant hutch on a snip of land–to a niece named Smith. In bad repair, though restorable, the log tollhouse, only one of that type on the Snickersville Pike, came down in the late 1950s.

James M. Mount who inherited one of Ezekial's old farms, Beaver Dam, in 1897, was the last of the Mount men in Loudoun. When he died in 1920, he was living in Purcellville and owned but a "small lot of land with a store-house thereon, known as Mountville." His wife Anne M. Mount, shortly sold the old store to William T. E. Bolen who had been running his competing store for a decade and a half.

As the village was a late-19th-century center for millwrights, it became the focus for veterinarians a generation later. Bluemont-area native Dr. Robert L. Humphrey practiced there in the early teens and after a stint in the army opened a practice at Creek Hill Farm, Mountville, in 1921. Dr. Humphrey, whose brother Frank practiced at Philomont, was the first long-time area veterinarian, a horse specialist, and his office at Creek Hill remained open until his death in 1954. His son, Dr. W. Rufus Humphrey, also practiced at the farm, 1945-1950, and after his military service moved to Sam Fred Road, and in 1955 to Mount Defiance. Dr. Robert L."Bob" Booth, who worked a year with the elder Dr. Humphrey at Creek Hill in 1935, moved to Valley View near Macsville, and was at his familiar Boley House by Glenwood Park in 1941. Dr. Booth began as an equestrian specialist, but with his heart on the farm, he switched to a bovine practice. He retired in 1985.

In 1954 at the instigation of Carl Furr, prominent Mountville horse-

PHOTO COURTESY ROBERT L. HUMPHREY JR.

William T. E. Bolen's Store, ca. 1955

man and farmer, the state agreed to macadamize the road to Pot House. Miss Charlotte Noland then halted the operation because she wanted her girls to be able to ride to Bolen's store to buy their candy and pop; a dirt road was easier on hooves than a rock road. Carl, who owned all the land about Camp Highroad, simply said, "No road, no [fox] hunting." Miss Charlotte for ever after would refer to the road as "Carl Furr's Boulevard."

By 1955 or so, after the closing of Will Bolen's post office and store, and until today, the highway department sign noting "Mountville" pointed to an empty church, closed school, store, butcher-shop, and soon-to-be-taken-down tollhouse.

But lest these closing comments give you an idea of a decaying neighborhood, in the past two decades the village has undergone a renaissance through the efforts of Jan Evans, who has acquired most of the Mount family's several farms; and Stanley Lickey, efficient farm manager of adjacent Delta Farm to Mountville's east. Jan has seen to it that such rarities as all the old village buildings—save for Jack Hibbs' butcher shop, beyond repair—have been well cared for. And she has even fixed up the old blacksmith shop and cattle scales.

Stanley has made certain that Delta, once the domain of another area kingpin, Benjamin Franklin Carter, has kept its one-room pre-Civil War school intact—as well as the farm's notable stone springhouse, slave quarters, and barn—and the original 18th century route of the old Mountain or Middle Road.

And out of sight, but not out of mind, Ezekial and Sarah Mount rest by a gnarled apple tree Mountville folk say was planted in that fall of 1814, within sight of the road they had turned.

Hibbs' Bridge

Its Trolls Were Hibbses

Little more than a mile northwest of Mountville, on the old Snickersville Pike, Loudoun Country's third oldest bridge spans Beaverdam Creek. Like its two older counterparts—the circa 1813 Turnpike span over Little River at Aldie, and the 1819 Ashby's Gap Turnpike Bridge over Goose Creek east of Upperville—its two stone arches are barrel-type. It was built sometime between 1819 and 1835.

In the late 1730s Loudoun's oldest westward road forded Beaverdam at the bridge site. Deeds then called the way the "Blue Ridge Road," leading to the 'Indian thoroughfare" at Williams's Gap (today's Snickers' Gap). By the close of the French and Indian War in 1763, the name Colchester Road came into use, as the way led east to the Occoquan River port of Colchester.

As Colchester declined late in the century, the name Mountain Road became prominent. An Anglican Mountain Chapel stood a half mile north of the bridge. Others called the way Middle Road, as it connected the Ashby's Gap Road and the Snickers' Gap Road. Others still called it Snickers' Road, because during Revolutionary times, Edward Snickers was responsible for its upkeep between the Mountain Chapel and the Shenandoah River.

In 1810 the State Legislature approved $20,000 for construction of the more-than-13-mile-long Snickers' Gap Turnpike between Aldie and Snickers' Ferry on the Shenandoah. Construction must have begun soon, because by 1813 deeds along the road mention the "new Snickers Gap Turnpike road." Clerks generally left the apostrophe off Snickers because they didn't know where to put it.

While some forty feet wide where the turnpike crossed, Beaverdam wasn't deep enough to warrant a bridge until after 1819. But the turnpike crossing was a good site for a mill, and here, by 1822, "Browns Mills...on the North side of the Beaverdam" was standing. Miller Samuel Brown owed William Hoge $1,127.50 that year, so he signed his property of 10 ¼ acres over to Hoge's benefit, with Mr. Brown still running the mill.

Then, sometime before December 1835, neighbor Uriel Glascock, owner of land on the south side of Beaverdam, decided to put up a sawmill less than 1,000 feet upstream from Mr. Brown's grist mill on the other side of the turnpike. As water in Beaverdam sometimes wasn't too plentiful, miller Brown complained and got the county court to condemn 3½ acres of Uriel Glascock's land. On Christmas Day, 1835, Brown was deeded a "parcel of land on the south side of the Beaverdam at the Bridge and on both sides of the Snickers Gap Turnpike road." This phrase is the first mention of the bridge in Loudoun records.

PHOTO COURTESY THOMAS BALCH LIBRARY

The early-19th-century Hibbs' Bridge over Beaver Dam Creek

Both mills must have had their problems, because trustee Daniel Janney sold them and the 1044 acres for only $1,391 to Griffith E. Thomas. Mr. Thomas, in turn, calling himself a "Yeoman of Loudoun County," sold "several contiguous lots, with the Merchant Mill and Saw Mill thereon, at the Beaver Dam Bridge on the Snickers Gap turnpike Road" to Samuel Megeath for $1,800 in August 1840. Then in February 1857, Sam Megeath and wife Mary Ann, sold the property for $1,500 to Stephen and William Hibbs, operators of the mill for some years. Their acquisition is described as "at the Beaverdam Bridge on the Snickers Gap turnpike Road consisting of Merchant Mill, saw mill, Dwelling House and two lots or parcels of land lying adjacent to said Merchant Mill."

Hibbs' Bridge it became, and here during the Civil War, Henry

Hibbs lived with his bride, Sarah Elizabeth Walker, whose family owned a tanyard a mile upstream. Elizabeth's sister, Charlotte Milhollen of Philomont, had a daughter Alice, who chose to stay with her aunt down at Hibbs'. Alice Walker Hendon's letter of September 21, 1919, is preserved among Walker Family records.

> General [Alfred E.] Pleasanton and staff had headquarters at the house of my Aunt, Sarah Elizabeth Hibbs, where I was staying at the time, and I can assure you it was not a very pleasant experience as the Confederate cavalry leader "Jeb" Stuart and General Pleasanton had a skirmish and the shells whizzed over the house and fell lost beyond.
>
> It did not last long as General Pleasanton soon moved on towards his objective in the Shenandoah Valley. I had many other experiences during the Civil War, some very sad and some amusing. Had it not been for the capture and execution of a member of John S. Mosby's detachment by a member band of Federal scouts, I would probably be writing you today under another name.
>
> I went to Washington City on a Wednesday last to see General Pershing and his soldier boys from overseas in the grand parade. It was a grand sight. Hence you see my span of life has extended through four wars in and against the United States. God grant it may never occur again.

A contingent of Major General Merritt's 1st Brigade probably took the measure of at least the merchant mill at Hibbs' on December 1, 1864, in the course of their infamous "Burning Raid." They might have spared the sawmill because the log yard spilled over into the Hibbs's front yard. If they did spare it, it was gone with the flood of May 1889. Carl Furr, remembering the area from the early 1890s recalled no mill, but remembers hearing "it washed away."

"Old Man Hibbs," as Henry was called in his later years, was a great cattle buyer and drover during postwar years. He would herd stock all the way to Baltimore. He had his schoolmate chum, Airmont's Lucien Powell, come down to Hibbs' to paint the bridge's underbelly, one of Powell's few Loudoun scenes. But the state concreted the archway in the late 1930s, part of its improvements to the Snickersville Pike.

Jack Hibbs, of the Leesburg Hibbses, also lived at the bridge after the war. Jack was a noted butcher. He'd kill a beef in summer, let it hang a day, then cut it up and wagon it out as far as Upperville. Uncle Jack, as everybody called him, liked his whiskey, and if a customer knew he wasn't going to be home when Jack came around, he'd leave a shot on the table. Uncle Jack left the bridge about 1912, moving on to butcher at Mountville, where he partnered with Will Bolen.

With Jack's departure, six Hibbses remained at the bridge: Henry's widow, Annie Decatur Hibbs and her three grown children, Loue, Clinton–formerly a clerk for Albert Milhollen at the Philomont store–and Stephen Decatur, better known as Bub and addicted to the jug that rode along in the produce wagon from Purcellville to Philomont..

Then there were the aging maiden aunts, Miss Cindy and Miss Eliza, finest quilters in the neighborhood, specialists in ocean-wave, sunburst, and log-cabin patterns. They charged five cents for every thread of cotton you gave them to work. They baby-sat Dick Lake of Philomont and would keep him happy with ginger cakes and a big ball of cotton thread of many colors. Whenever he could, Dick's father, Francis, would bring the aunts a four-horse-wagon load of wood, corn, and feed for the hogs and cows.

After Francis died in 1909, Dick would always try to visit the sisters. He remembers that once Miss Cindy was laid up for a few days and told him, "I have never been to Leesburg and I've never seen a moving train."

When Miss Cindy died, about 1916, a cousin told the preacher at the funeral, the Reverend Frank Ridgeway of Roszell Chapel at Philomont, that Miss Cindy had given her a bag of pennies, tied up in a handkerchief, to pay for the occasion.

Stephen Decatur Hibbs, last of the Hibbses of Beaverdam, died in 1943. His 12 ¼ acres "improved by an old house" was sold at auction for $1,000 that November 15. His estate was worth $128.10. The house, two-story log with shingled roof, was taken down in 1947.

Agricultural Institute

From Bitzer, To Belcher, To Beagles

In Montgomery County, Virginia, there are two historical markers, one at the east end of Christiansburg, the other at the approach to the Virginia Tech campus at Blacksburg. Both markers refer to VPI [Virginia Polytechnic Institute] with a braggadocio so typical of the old markers: "Its founding, [1872] marked the beginning of scientific, agricultural and industrial instruction in Virginia."

This statement is not true. As early as the late 1830s, Miss Margaret Mercer was teaching agriculture and science at her Belmont Academy in Loudoun County, and some twenty years before Virginia Tech there was the Loudoun County Agricultural and Chemical Institute. Loudoun A & C may very well have been the oldest institution of its type in the United States.

Photo courtesy Thomas Balch Library

The original Agricultural Institute, built by Harmon Bitzer

The years between 1854 and 1858 saw the beginning of the first three agricultural colleges established in the United States: Massachusetts Agricultural College, Michigan Agricultural College, and State College of Pennsylvania. The only readily available information about the three I could obtain was for the State College, founded as Farmers' High School in 1855, with the first "college" classes beginning in 1859. The institution is now Pennsylvania State University. Loudoun Agricultural and Chemical Institute predates Penn State by at least two years.

The first reference I could find to what was commonly called the Agricultural Institute, or the Institute, is Yardley Taylor's 1853 *Map of Loudoun County*, surveyed in 1852. On this map, by a building symbol at the location where the present Institute Building now stands, are the words "Agricultural Institute." That this institution did not exist for many years prior to 1852 is evidenced by Yardley Taylor's not mentioning its presence in his *Memoir of Loudoun County* that accompanied the map. Mr. Taylor, an avid horticulturist would have written about the facility had it been a fixture.

The Institute probably was the idea of Loudoun educator Benjamin Hyde Benton, who, at his family's New Lisbon plantation (now Huntland) near Pot House, had founded New Lisbon Institute, a private boarding school for boys. In defiance of state law, Professor Benton and Margaret Harrison Benton taught family slaves to read and write. He was also active in the Loudoun Education Society, a group that campaigned for a county public-school system. During the Civil War, Mr. Benton was dismissed from Long Branch Baptist Church at Halfway for demeaning the Confederacy in several public addresses.

A partner in the venture was Harmon Bitzer, an area builder. He constructed the stuccoed-stone four-story Institute building, then the largest structure in Loudoun County. By the spring of 1854, however, he had left the partnership for reasons not known. When asked about Mr. Bitzer's role in the partnership, Elizabeth O. Carter of Oatlands said in an 1868 deposition:

> I can only state that Benton & Gulick succeeded Benton, Gulick, and Bitzer…There was also a contract beween B. H. Benton, J. H. Gulick, and Harmon Bitzer to carry on the Loudoun Institute. Mr. Bitzer came before me and stated that he had never done anything as a partner having withdrawn from the firm shortly after the date of the contract having Benton and Gulick carrying on the concern. They did carry it on for some time…

James H. Gulick, the third partner of Loudoun A & C, handled the business side of the venture. It was he who bought the land, 421 acres for $4,821 in 1846. The tract, largely wooded—hence the near-bargain price of about $1.50 an acre—had been part of President James Monroe's Oak Hill estate. The sellers were Maria and Samuel S. Gouverneur, who lived in New York, the daughter and son-in-law of the deceased president.

A September 29, 1854 advertisement in the *Leesburg Washingtonian*, submitted to the paper on June 2, gives first mention of the academics of the Loudoun County Agricultural and Chemical Academy, managed by "Benton & Gulick," Aldie. The ad mentions that "instruction is given in all branches of mathematics and science useful to the farmer and the man of business," with "practical application of their studies to the everyday affairs of life." Curricula included "quantity and strength of materials used for building and other purposes, surveying farms, leveling water courses, laying out roads, making maps, mechanical drawing, calculations required in the construction of machinery," with advance students taught "how to prepare pure chemicals, analyze soils, minerals, marls."

The advertisement closed by noting, "Buildings are new and commodious. The laboratory is conveniently arranged for all the manipulations in qualitative analysis, and the location has all the advantages of purity of water, salubrity of atmosphere and beauty of scenery."

A June 15, 1885, advertisement in the *Washingtonian* noted courses of instruction "varied to suit the farmer, the merchant, the engineer." Sessions began the first of October and closed the first of the following August. Tuition was $200 a year with students in the "classical department" paying $20 a session extra. The ad further noted, "Sons of Preachers and Editors are charged only $150 per session." It closed by advising, "Farmers can have their soils analyzed and teachers and students can obtain pure chemical tests at the establishment."

That *Washingtonian* issue mentioned that on June 8, a number of prominent agricultural experts and farmers visited The Institute to inspect the apparatus and grounds and to interview the students, "who were rigidly examined by a Mr. Belcher of Vermont in the several branches of mathematics and science." The Reverend G. W. Harris of Frederick County and Samuel Benjamin Taylor Caldwell of Wheatland, Loudoun County, spoke. Mr. Caldwell could readily appreciate the $50 discount given to sons of editors, for he was a veteran newspaperman and founder of the important Leesburg newspaper, *The Genius of Liberty*. In the evening, Mr. Belcher gave "a highly interesting lecture" on "physical geography." The article concluded: "The visitors expressed themselves as highly pleased with the general arrangements, the facilities afforded, the method of instruction, the progress of the students, and the workmanship and finish of the apparatus made on the premises."

By 1860 the Institute was no more for it probably had become a casualty of the 1857 depression. James Hixson Gulick offered its 117 acres at public sale, January 1, 1861, "The Loudoun Institute Property" contained "Buildings new, large and commodious, well calculated for a Boarding-school, a shoe or other factory, or a private residence. It has a young orchard of between 400 and 500 choice fruit trees and almost every other convenience that makes a place desirable." Mr. Gulick's 427-acre "Goose Creek Farm" was also for sale.

With war clouds overhead, Mr. Gulick was unable to sell. Confederate Major John S. Mosby notes on June 17, 1863:

> "It was a very hot day and we had stopped a while to rest under the shade of some trees, and refresh ourselves with buttermilk at the house of a farmer named Gulick. Presently we heard artillery firing over toward Aldie, which indicated a collision of the enemy's cavalry with ours. In an instant, every man was mounted. From a commanding position on the mountain, which we reached in a few minutes, I could see clouds of dust rising on every road."

The battle, taking place a mile and one-half south on the Snickersville Pike, was one of the war's costliest, often called the "hardest-fought small cavalry battle" of the Civil War. Briefly, the Yanks rode up the pike, the Rebs, down. Among the 424 killed, wounded, or missing were 178 of the 1st Massachusetts Cavalry. The marker there today was put up in 1889 by the Curtis family of Boston. In gratitude to the Dallas Furr's family, who lived on the property, the Curtises presented the Furrs with a Salem rocker.

After James Gulick's death in 1867, the 117 acres was again up for sale and retained the name "the Institute Farm" for many years, with the larger tract, now down to 375 acres, called the "Gulick Farm." Both became the property of Isabella Skinner Turner, and upon her death were sold as a parcel to "The Institute Corporation," for $11,500 on February 16, 1916.

That year the old Agricultural Institute became headquarters of the National Beagle Clubs, with the corporation renting the property to the NBC for one dollar a year. The Institute Corporation was, in reality, five gentlemen, all of whom gave their residence as New York City when they incorporated that January 27. Their offices may have been in New York, but most were from New England. All–James W. Appleton, president; George P. Post, vice president; Ramsay Turnbull, secretary-treasurer; and Arthur S. Burden and John S. Phipps–were devotees of a new sport known as beagling.

Beagling is a foot sport and the prey–rarely caught–is a cottontail rabbit. Into the 1980s there were brace trials, run the first weekend in April. One hound was pitted against another, and judges followed on horseback, observing the accuracy of their pursuit of the rabbit.

Then there are pack trials, held in April and the first week of November, where three-, four-, and eight-couple packs (six to 16 hounds) work together as a unit pursuing the rabbit. A huntsman decked in blue starts them off with brass horn, and whippers-in keep the hounds together. Again, judges on horseback follow, looking for the pack that pursues its game accurately and enthusiastically. The special stake held in November, pits two hounds, one pair from each pack, against each other in an attempt to find the best individual hound. Similar outings with bassets are now fixtures in late April and late October.

The beaglers had their beginnings in Boston with the founding of the National Beagle Club in 1889. In 1892, Mr. Appleton, master of the Waldingfield Beagles, of Ipswich, Massachusetts, became president; a post he retained until his death in 1942. The NBC held its first brace trials at Hyannis, Massachusetts, November 3, 1890 and the first pack trials in 1892 at Nanuet, Long Island. For a number of years the trials were held at various farms in the Northeast. Then, following the lead of Harry Worcester Smith's New England foxhunters, they came to Loudoun County in 1910.

At first the beaglers held the trials at various farms, boarding at Pemberton, the old Berkeley home in Aldie, and then in tents on the Institute property. With these beaglers was C. Oliver Iselin Jr.'s Wolver Pack from Middleburg, founded in 1913, Virginia's oldest pack. After the death of James Appleton in 1942, Mr. Iselin became NBC president until 1971. Also with the first Loudoun trials were hounds from Lyttleton A. Turner's Glenstone Pack of Aldie. Mr. Turner didn't run his beagles at the trials, but sold many to the other packs. His daughter Georgiana attended the first official trials of 1916, and every trial from 1935 until 1977.

With the 10 old dormitory rooms of the institute not quite livable, log cabins were built for the pack owners. The first cabins went up in 1917, built for Boston's Chetwood Smith, James Appleton, and George Post. They cost $500. The newest of the old 11, built in 1971 cost $7,000. Since 1972, seven more have joined that lucky number.

Two of the 18 cabins are not log, but are of board-and-batten, and they are the "squaw cabins," put up in the late 1920s at the request of proper Bostonian, James Appleton. He asserted that women did not belong on the property, and the beagle trials began as stag affairs. However, the twenties of F. Scott Fitzgerald brought in the wives, and the club built a "Squaw Camp" of two cabins, 500 yards to the northwest of the men's quarters. By the late thirties, attitudes changed a bit, and the squaw camp cabins joined the log ones.

Among the famous packs of years past were Richard V. N. Gambrill's Vernon Somerset Pack from Far Hills, New Jersey, winners in various classes from 1923–1925, and through the 1930s. Then there was William Newbold Ely's Treweryn Pack from Gwynedd Valley, Pennsylvania, begun in 1924, taken over in 1929 by David B. Sharp Jr., and a winner in 1938 and several times in the 1940s and 1950s.

PHOTO COURTESY THOMAS BALCH LIBRARY

The cabins at The Institute

In 1964 the Treweryn Pack merged with Rebecca Lanier Trimpi's 1927 Nantucket Pack, a steady winner in the fifties, to form the Nantucket-Treweryn Pack. Miss Lanier, granddaughter of Georgia poet Sidney Lanier, in 1955 married David Sharp, who since the early forties had been a director of the National Beagle Club of America. Subsequent presidents of the club have been L. Stockton Illoway, Master of the Ardrossan Beagles, Villanova, Pennsylvania, and today's president, Richard P. "Rick" Roth, Master of the Bear Lane Beagles, Frenchtown, New Jersey.

Sixteen of the 28 registered beagle packs in the U. S. were represented at the April 2002 pack trials.Virginia, which until the 1940s had only one registered pack, the Wolver, now has nine, more than any other state. Only the Wolver Pack is from Loudoun, for Nantucket-Treweryn moved to Berryville in Clarke County. The other local pack is Middleburg-Orange County, from The Plains in Fauquier.

Sixteen of the National Beagle Club's 21 events during 2002 were held at the old Agricultural Institute. While I didn't attend any that year, I've stood on the grassy outcrops of the club's 502 acres on many a misty and chilly morning.

Solitude is one's reward for awaiting the rabbit and pursuing beagles. And if there is another need, it is the warming cup of coffee in the basement dining hall of The Institute. The pot might have once been poured by Mr. Benton himself.

Laceyville

Uncle Josh Razed The Old Motel

Back in the 1730s and 1740s, three men dominated the Fairfax County Courthouse gang. Two of them, Amos Janney and William West, lived in the rich lands of western Fairfax, which in 1757 became Loudoun County. The third, Catesby Cocke, was clerk of the court, who while forced by his profession to live close to the courthouse, dabbled in the rich properties to the west. Cocke's specialty was watching for unpaid rents. When rents were unpaid for three years, deeds to the properties became null and void. He then notified the agents of Thomas, sixth Lord Fairfax and asked if "his lordship" would consider regranting the lands to one Catesby Cocke. Once regranted, Cocke sold the property shortly thereafter for profit.

Messrs. Janney and West were Lord Fairfax's surveyors, and unofficially they divided their western domain. Janney knew the shape of every white oak north of Goose Creek, and West could take measure of treetops to the south. There was little surprise, then, when William West took up land at the most enviable crossroads in western Fairfax, that of the Carolina and Colchester Roads, respectively the main north-south and east-west roads in all the Fairfax Proprietary. It was here that he built West's Ordinary, most famous stop-over in frontier Virginia. If a westward traveler chose not to stop here, Mr. West was also proprietor of Bacon Fort Tavern, 11 miles up the Colchester Road.

Miss Alice Maude Ewell, historian and writer from Haymarket, described West's Ordinary in its last days as a

> Low, long rambling building, a combination of log and stone. The weatherboard front was logs, the back more substantial stone. The chimneys, also of stone, were massive. A metallic roof replaced the old one of riven shingles. This old roof of shingles was set with a row of quaint dormer windows which the metallic roof lacked. Sixty feet long and forty feet wide, the building, with attic, contained eight great oak beamed rooms on the ground floor, in two rows front and back opening into each other without entries. There were enormous fireplaces, eight feet wide in which hung the spit and kettles.
>
> The house looks its century and a half. Its rooms suggest old-fashioned simplicity and confidence. No standing at arms' length in those days of primitive hospitality. Even in later times, when Mme. Nellie Custis made this a favorite stopping place between memorial Woodlawn and her valley home, she probably shared the common sitting and dining room nor lost

dignity thereby. At one end of the building, near the airy pump, was a stone house, thick walls, but now in ruins. At the other (also a heap of stones) was the great outer kitchen. Its fireplace may still be measured. As usual, it was the biggest of all, the breadth being fully eight feet. For all the roasting and boiling that doubtless went on, there would still be room for those 'end benches,' so celebrated, where we were told the oldest and youngest darkies toasted their shins in ante-bellum days. With the mountains so near, it is likely they also roasted many a quart of chestnuts.

Miss Ewell's observations were backed up with photos she took. West's, built before 1748, looked exactly like today's typical motel. On April 12, 1748, 16-year-old George Washington, returning from a surveying expedition in the Shenandoah Valley, noted in one of his first diary entries: "We did get over Wms. Gap that Night and as low as Wm. Wests in Fairfax County 18 Miles from ye Top of ye Ridge. This day see a Rattled Snake ye first we had seen in all our Journey."

PHOTO COURTESY THOMAS BALCH LIBRARY

West's Ordinary, a rare photo, and all that's left of Lacey's

As one of the gentry, West kept his ordinary on a private basis and didn't apply for a public license until 1754. When Loudoun was formed three years later, he applied for renewal of his license at the May 1758, County Court. The court approved: "Ordered that a License be granted to William West to keep an Ordinary at his House on Fruit Hill for one Year."

On July 31, 1769, George Washiington, then Colonel Washington, Mrs. Washington, and her daughter Patsy Custis, lodged at the ordinary, which now belonged to William's son, Charles West, on their way to Berkeley Springs, then known as Bath. After a month-and-a half sojourn, they returned and again stopped at West's. In May of 1772, Washington spent two more nights at West's and in March 1774, Washington was West's guest for several days. That November, as executor of Colonel John Mercer's estate, Washington held an auction at West's Ordinary to dispose of Mercer's Bull Run lands.

Alice Maude Ewell, who had seen West's guest registers then called "day books," recalled that a veritable who's who of colonial America passed the nights there: Thomas, sixth Lord Fairfax, General Edward Braddock, Daniel Boone, Louise Philippe of France and his two brothers, the Duke of Montpensier and the Count de Berijealais, Nellie Custis, Marquis de Lafayette, and the French naturalist, Constantin Volney. Early in the 20th century, one of the Riticor ladies found one of the day books in the attic of West's. She told Fannie Watson Utterback of Smithfield, up towards Watson, of her find. As Mrs. Utterback was related to the Wests and the Laceys, she asked for and received the day book. Upon her death it passed to Francis Watson of near Haymarket in Prince William. Mr. Watson felt the book should remain in Loudoun, and gave it to the Loudoun Historical Society. Not a good idea. It's been lost for a quarter century.

In 1769, the year the ordinary passed to Charles West, a second building appeared by the crossroads, one you would hardly expect in that situation—a church. That September 2, for one shilling, William West deeded to Benjamin Hutchison one-half acre "in the forks of the Roads leading to William's Gap in the Blue Ridge and to Leesburg," noting "the present meeting House now built" to make "use of a meeting house and School house for any School master approved by the said William West and the Majority of the Neighbours who are Customers to the said Master to teach School."

This was the first Little River Baptist Church, named, as was custom, for the nearest large stream. That fiery preacher, David Thomas, organized its first congregation, later led by pastor Richard Major. By 1772, however, the teacher did not suit either his "customers" or the Wests. As stipulated in the deed, if such dissatisfaction occurred, the property was to revert to the Wests. Again, the teacher might have been entirely suitable, but the location was probably somewhat raucous, in that neighbor Joseph Hutchison complained about the interminable loud singing.

So that March 2, 1772, the congregation moved more than a mile down the Carolina Road to a quiet, peaceful location. Samuel Wyckoff sold one acre to John Lewis and Joseph Hutchison, in trust, for the denomination of Anabaptists for 20 shillings. The land was "for the use and purpose of Erecting and Building a meetinghouse." By 1814, with the church membership coming from Manassas to Upperville, a brick church was built. It was replaced in 1890 by a frame building built by Jake Watson for $576.25. Fire destroyed that church in 1971, and once again Little River was rebuilt as a brick church.

Returning up-road to the ordinary, Thomas West helped his father Charles run the ordinary during the 1770s. In later years of that decade, a relation, Joseph Lacey, took over its management. Charles West's will of January 29, 1777, gave to his daughter Elizabeth "all my land belonging to the public House where Joseph Lacey now lives also including the plantation where I now live." Landlord Charles West was now an officer in the Continental forces, and proprietor Lacey was not very happy with the English term "ordinary," so he changed the establishment's name to "tavern," a more patriotic designation.

Elizabeth West, meanwhile, did not accept the gift of the plantation, and on September 19, 1780, Major Charles West sold its 227 acres, described as "under the Bull run mountain and wherein the said Charles West now lives," to a Pennsylvanian, Thomas Schofield. The sale price was £500 ($1,665). Ten years later, for the same price, the Schofields sold the tract, now grown to 371 acres, to Joseph Lacey, keeper of West's ordinary for at least 13 years. George Washington recorded his last stop at the old tavern on June 4, 1788, when he dined with "one Lacey."

A few years later, when construction began on the U. S. Capitol, the knell sounded for Lacey's. Instead of travelers taking the Carolina Road south, they detoured east to see the seat of the new government. By these days, the prolific Laceys and kin had placed their name upon the neighborhood, and Laceyville became the common designation for lands between the Little River neighborhood and Aldie. Because Joseph Lacey died in 1800 or 1801, he did not see the final demise of his tavern. In 1802 the Little River Turnpike Company was chartered, and by 1806 its macadamized road had bypassed the tavern. Turnpike directors thought it more important to build straightway to reach the

Mercer-family mill on Little River.

Lacey's old tavern continued under management of Stephen and Ozpah Beard, who on September 26, 1816, bought the property from four maiden daughters of Joseph Lacey: Huldah, Naomi, Ruth, and Tacey. The Beards' son Jonathan was a bachelor, and by April 6, 1855, when he inherited the family property, the tavern's role as one of the most famous rural stopovers of colonial times was history.

Just as the name "White Pump" followed the demise of Bacon Fort, the name Ish's Tanyard followed that of Lacey's Tavern. Ish's, its house still standing where today's Route 15 intersects the old Carolina Road was one of two plantation houses of Charles West, the other being a stone house on the hill closer to the tavern, gone long before 1900. Here in 1792, Jacob Ish, first of his family in Loudoun, bought land from John Moore, and in 1796 increased his holdings by purchasing some of Thomas Schofield's land (originally West's). In 1807 Jacob Ish bought again, this time from Elijah Rittaker and wife Nancy, a daughter of John Moore. According to Gertrude and Edna Ish, their forbearers helped William Benton build Oak Hill in 1821-1823, but the fame of the Ish family rests on their long history as tanners. Jacob Ish was the first, and Richard Ish, of the Civil War period, the last.

With the Ishes off to war and the tannery vacant, a young wholesale grocer in Alexandria by the name of Sidney Bruin enlisted in the Southern army. When the enlisting sergeant found out he had experience as a tanner, they told him to go to Ish's Tanyard and get it going again. That Sidney Bruin did, until he was picked up by David Hunter's Federal field forces, ostensibly looking for Mosby's men, but really picking up every man of military age. Operations at the tannery presumably stopped when manufactured leather goods came into vogue in the 1880s.

Before 1930, Miss Ewell remembered most locals thought that West's Ordinary was actually George Neavil's, down in Auburn, Fauquier County. In those days, the average person did not go into the courthouse and hunt up old deeds. Then, she says, Fairfax Harrison, preparing his epic *Landmarks of Old Prince William*, set them straight. But when *Landmarks* came out in 1924, only a scant 150 copies were issued. One of those copies should have reached Josh Riticor. He owned the old tavern then and didn't have the slightest notion of its history. He also didn't know Miss Ewell. But he did know that the old stone and beams in the ordinary had value, and he wanted to build a tenant house. So to get a few materials, he decided to tear down West's.

Tom Fendall, county surveyor at the time, and a man interested in old things, happened to overhear Uncle Josh's plans. Tom also acted as farm manager for Rockland's Henry Rust, and knowing of Mr. Rust's interest in history–and also that they had the funds to buy–he told Henry Rust of Josh's plans. Mr. Rust proffered an amount to Mr. Riticor far beyond the building's market value.

But Uncle Josh was stubborn. He tore down West's in 1925, and in its place built a frame bungalow now in its 72nd year. Before 1925 not many had thought much about preserving the county's old buildings, but the needless destruction of West's changed things. Everybody loved old Uncle Josh, but not many could forgive him.

West's Ordinary, another view ILLUSTRATION COURTESY THOMAS BALCH LIBRARY

St. Louis

If You Were A Baptist You Lived Here

When the talented and likable equestrienne Mrs. Archibald Cary Randolph moved to Oakley, near Upperville, she was in need of a cook. A friend commented there was a good one in St. Louis. "I'll airmail a letter to her immediately," said Mrs. Randolph. Only in Fauquier and Loudoun could such a comment provoke smiles. The prospective cook was not in Missouri, but just down the road.

How did St. Louis, with some 200 persons, the largest black village in Loudoun County and the horse and hunt country of America, get its name? Some weeks after I offered some theories in my original 1980 articles on the village, Melvin A. Warren, former carrier of the rural Route 2 called me and told me he remembered.

Phil McQuay, the long-time St. Louis storekeeper was a great talker, Mr. Warren recalled, and they often chatted when Mr. Warren stopped to deliver mail to the store. Phil told Melvin that after the Civil War one of the McQuays went to St. Louis, Missouri, and there spent several years. And as they used to say, he came home to die. The rest of the McQuays dubbed the home-comer "Little St. Louis," and the name soon was applied to the McQuay's settlement.

The first mention of St. Louis in a Loudoun County deed book bears the date May 26, 1891. Lot No. 4, of Emily and Bedford Glascock, in "Little St. Lewis," had been sold to Dan M. Robinson. The subdivision Little St. Lewis had been surveyed and mapped prior to 1881 for Thomas Glascock, well-heeled and of the gentry, who owned several large holdings in upper Fauquier and Loudoun. Beginning in 1881 he began to sell lots, generally one acre for $20, to his former slaves and the former slaves of the Carters, Dulanys, Gochnauers, and other landed area families.

Ann Gillison bought what appears to be the first lot in 1881. Charles and James McQuay bought lots in 1889. None of these deeds, however, calls the subdivision St. Louis or any other name. Neither does Thomas Glascock's 1884 will, which passes the subdivision on to wife Emily W. Glascock and son, Bedford Glascock.

By 1900 St. Louis was home to many of the blacks owning acreage in Mercer district. Gustavus Cook owned 5 acres, Joseph McQuay

7, Arch Strother 11, Charles McQuay 14, C. J. Howard 16, Stiles Carter 18, and Garner Peters 30. The homes of Howard and Strother were assessed at $420 and $400, surpassed only by the Reverend Richard Dawson's handsome brick house in Middleburg. Whites called the McQuays and others "High Society" because they owned property and had been there a long time.

Without once mentioning that he was describing a Negro village, the *Loudoun Telephone*'s reporter, dateline "St. Louis," December 9th 1889, presented this description:

> Here you will find as good, whole-souled and hospitable people as ever lived. It can boast of but one church (Baptist), one school, and one store. The school, I find, for want of stimulus, is not as progressive as I had expected; yet, with patient and continuous work, I think it may be brought to par with mediocrity.

In a sense the village was the "black" Middleburg, even replete with its own "St. Louis Colored Colt Show," officially chartered in 1898 "to hold exhibitions of horses and colts and to manage and conduct contests of speed and jumping; and such other tests of excellence in horses and colts...but no gambling of any sort shall be allowed." Shares sold for five dollars, and among the officers were Mountville's Lloyd Champe and Welbourne's John Howard. That the horse show never made the many Hunt Country publications did not deter Charles McQuay. He cleared his ground, and from two to four days each August there were steeplechases and showings of yearlings and colts. Admission was a quarter.

Blacks used to say that if you were a Methodist you lived in Willisville and if you were a Baptist you lived in St. Louis. With the election of Governor Philip W. McKimmey in 1889, the old-line Democrats were once more in power, and blacks foresaw the coming of segregation. After subtle hints that they were no longer welcome at Ebenezer, Middleburg and Upperville Baptist, they formed their own congregation. They organized the still-standing St. Louis School, built before April 1877, and the earliest public building and land in Mercer District bought for the Negro race. The congregation first met at the school and various homes under the guidance of Elder Wormly Hughes.

On December 1, 1891, for $30, church trustees George Berryman, Robert McQuay Sr., and Jack Short bought an acre of land for the "St. Louis New School Baptist Church." That deed was the first of record to spell the village name correctly. And as with so many black churches of the period, the building's date stone is a capsule of history: "M. Z. B. C. Built by Rev. M. B. Strother, July 30, 1893. Rebuilt by Rev. T. Johnson Oct. 6, 1929." The "rebuilt," referred to the present church, for sometime before 1919 the original building, located east of the present church, and labeled "Burnt Church"—its local designation—on this book's map, burned. The congregation then met at the school until the open-belfreyed and Gothic windowed Mount Zion Baptist Church was completed in 1929.

The Reverend Moses B. Strother pastored at both the old church and school, and about 1920, he was followed by the Reverend Thornton Johnson. Elders at the century's turn, and leaders of the area's black Baptist community, were Shelton Allen, Cedrick Short, Robert McQuay Sr., and Alfred Moore. In modern times, the Reverends John Paul Nicholas, Thomas Procter, and Allen Baltimore were the Zion Church pastors.

PHOTO COURTESY *COURAGE, MY SOUL*

Mount Zion Baptist Church, St. Louis

At the schoolhouse which had doubled as the church for a decade or so, remembered teachers were Mattie McQuay Berryman, Anna Gaskins, Grace and Clarence Murray from the Bull Run Mountain, Powell Gibson, and Armistead Smith and his son, Alfonso Smith. Each day the Smiths walked eight miles back and forth along the old road that forded Goose Creek at Millville, to and from their home at Middleburg. Terry Gaskins Colbert who taught at St. Louis about 70 years ago, recalls that the school was so crowded she could hardly count the children. There were always at least 40 in the one room.

By the early 1940s there were sometimes 50 students, and the older children attended school in a classroom set up in Phil McQuay's store. Under the leadership of Dr. Maurice Edmead, St. Louis and Middleburg parents asked the school board to relieve overcrowding at their schools. Dr. Edmead was the black physician from Middleburg who dispelled thoughts that blacks would not go to a black doctor because "how could a black know anything about medicine?"

With the end of World War II, the school board listened, and they bought 19½ acres in St. Louis from William K. Benton for $1,000. The acreage marked a record for a Loudoun public school. On March 31, 1948, a new six-room school opened with 185 students from the old St. Louis School, Grant School in Middleburg, and Marble Quarry School on Sam Fred Road. Pupils filled five rooms. But the school wasn't big enough for all, and first and second graders continued to go to school at Marble Quarry and at Middleburg's Shiloh Baptist Church. Augustus Lacey, who had taught at Grant School, was the first principal.

Combined PTAs from the old schools chose the name Banneker for the new school. Benjamin Banneker, the 18th century mathematician and astronomer had also helped survey the boundaries of the District of Columbia. The name, however, didn't come without a fight. The school board thought Mercer District School a "nice name," and only relented after the county N. A. A. C. P., led by Middleburg's no-nonsense contractor, William McKinley Jackson, threatened to take the matter to court.

St. Louis, by the turn of this century, had more than 100 people, but it had no post office. Yet it was far bigger than three of the four villages around it that did—Welbourne, Atoka, and Leithton. Blacks just didn't have the congressional clout to get a post office going.

St. Louis also never appeared on an official state road map; it never appeared on a county road map. Only "Phillips Corner" appeared at the crossroads of today's St. Louis and Welbourne Roads on county road maps of the 1930s. Annie Phillips lived at the corner, and sold handiwork in her home.

Before 1920 or so, most of the blacks in St. Louis worked in white homes, but the growing interest in blooded horses and the building of what later became the Middleburg Training Track, for Katherine Elkins Hitt in the early 1920s, changed that. Her Homeland estate track was within an easy walk of St. Louis. By the Depression many blacks were employed in the horse industry. The trend continued to 1954, when Paul Mellon of nearby Rokeby in Fauquier, bought and enlarged the track complex, aptly called by Kitty Slater, historian of the horsy set, "a combined primary, elementary, and preparatory school for thoroughbreds before they enter the higher education of the nation's racing ovals."

Some blacks worked elsewhere. Jim Anderson, a 1920s organizer of the Colored Colt Show ran the local dance hall, known as Anderson's Hall. He had it built in the early 1920s just across from Phil McQuay's store. He had hoped to have movies there, but that never came about. Dances were held on Saturday evenings, and he charged 50 cents a couple to pay the bands–Pogue's "Orchestra" from Washington, D. C., was a treat. But like the Colt Show, by 1930 the dances were gone. Mrs. Hitt bought the building, had it torn down, and sold the land back to the church.

Other village enterprises lingered on. Phil McQuay's store, a fixture since about 1916, closed in 1961. There were two other short-lived stores in the 1940s. Wallace Robinson had a store in one room of his home until it burned. In the 1950s Louise Grant had a store in her home. There was never a public smith in the village; old Will Warner at Welbourne was just too good, and it was certainly worth the four-mile round trip.

Willisville

A Village For Methodists And Gaskins

Born of former slaves, Willisville, like its sister communities, Howardsville and St. Louis, grew up on lands first rented, then bought, from the old masters. The bonds uniting black and white were rooted in stories such as those concerning "Uncle" Garner, Garner Peters in later years (Blacks did not legally have surnames until 1866), butler for the Dulanys of Welbourne.

Uncle Garner rode up to the manor house and told his master, Colonel Richard Henry Dulany, to escape. "Yankees are coming! Yankees are coming!" he yelled. A few hours after Colonel Dulany galloped off, the Yankees returned and showed the Colonel's stained tunic to Mr. Garner and the Dulany children. "I know the difference between pokeberry juice and blood," Garner replied. Dulany had doffed the tunic as a ruse.

Another time when Federal marauders emptied the Welbourne meat house, they commandeered wagons and made Garner drive them south to the Ashby's Gap Turnpike (today's Route 50). Garner "accidentally" upset the wagons in swollen Pantherskin Creek, later saying that if his people couldn't have meat, nobody could.

No stories appear to survive of the persons for whom Willisville takes its name. Heuson and Lucinda Willis had possibly been owned by Townsend L. Seaton of Catesby plantation, just south of the present village. On November 7, 1874, Mr. Seaton and his wife, Mary, deeded a cabin and 3.75 acres to Heuson Willis for $100–a bargain. The deed noted Lucinda Willis, possibly Heuson's wife, as living on the land. The Willis homeplace still stands, log and weatherboard, just west of the old store and is lived in by Mack Gaskins.

They used to say that if you were black and a Baptist you lived in St. Louis, and if you were black and a Methodist you lived in Willisville. The church, used by many Christian faiths for several years, began its history shortly after the Civil War and was organized by 1868. That August, Lieutenant Sidney B. Smith, head of the Freedmen's Bureau office in Middleburg, spoke to a delegation of "colored people in the vicinity of R. H. Dulany's." They wanted a neighborhood school. Lieutenant Smith granted their request and appropriated $150 to build the school and to fund it for a year. On October 1, John A. Carter deeded half an acre to George Evans, Garner Peters, and Benjamin Berry, "trustees for a schoolhouse and lot for exclusive use and benefit of young colored persons and children." The price was $40–an expensive lot considering that an acre usually sold for $20. The deed noted: "School house may be used on Sabbath days for the exclusive benefit of colored persons and for holding religious worship on Sabbath days for the colored population of the neighborhood."

Later that month, Lieutenant Smith wrote that the building was being constructed by George Evans, "a very reliable and worthy colored man to whom I turned the $150."

That was two years before the beginnings of public education in Loudoun County, and during this time when poor and middle-class whites had no schools to attend, there were three Middleburg-area schools for black children: the one at Antioch Church sponsored by the Freedmen's Bureau; Elias "Yankee" Smith's school at Boxwood, south of Middleburg; and the Willisville School.

Photo courtesy Thomas Balch Library

The 1919 Willisville School

In 1908 an 18-year-old Anna Shorts Gaskins began a 43-year teaching career at $25 a month at the Willisville School. She is remembered as an excellent teacher who was not adverse to giving a child a swat if he was out of line. But Mrs. Gaskins was a slight woman, and so she'd jump up and down because she couldn't hit very hard. Each day Mrs. Gaskins began school be reciting "The Lord's Prayer," and there would always be a Thanksgiving and Christmas program and a Santa Claus.

By 1884 the Willisville Church had become Methodist, and for $50 Lucinda Willis sold a half acre to the church for a parsonage. Church trustees at the time were John Howard of Howardsville, John Moore,

John H. Strother, Robert Brent, John Lewis, Calvin Nickens, Peter Webb, Jacob McKenzie and James Addison. The location was noted as on the road "from Millsville to the colored School house." The precise land was noted as in "Millsville," possibly a misrepresentation of Willisville, for Millville, an old mill village on Goose Creek, was a good four miles to the east. Other church trustees in the 19th century were George Brewer and Adolphus Hampton. Pastors, for whom we have no first names, were The Reverends Holland, Curtis, Carpenter, Waters, Meredith, and Love.

In 1917 the Willisville Church and School burned. For seven years services were held under trees in fair weather and at Fannie Dulany Lemmon's cottage at Welbourne when the weather was unpleasant. The children went to school at St. Louis and were taught by Mrs. Gaskins.

The Mercer District School Board would not build a new school unless the land was deeded to the school board. So at a June 1, 1919, church trustees' meeting, chaired by Moses Peters, the trustees, Mr. Peters, Lucius Gaskins, Frank Henderson, and Dorsey Warner, gave the land to the board. That fall the new Willisville School was built, and about 1933, with the influx of federal funds, it became a two-roomer.

Willisville's store dates from about 1912. It was first run by Harry Howard and wife Marie. Henry Grantland took over in the late 1920s, and during the 1940s and until about 1954 the business was run by Phil McQuay, the St. Louis merchant. Henry Jackson closed the business in the late 1960s.

Willisville's blacksmith shop was out of town, near the old Welbourne Post Office on Quaker Lane. Will Warner had the business at the turn of the century and Thomas Lee Sacra in the teens. After Sacra left for Marshall in 1921, William Smith became smith at 'The Welbourne Shop.' He remained there, remembered for his fine craft, until his death in the late 1940s.

Perhaps Willisville's first business was one well known by black society in Washington. Delia Howard's boarding house still stands, lived in by Ann Lee, behind Miss Howard's grandson's old store. The boarding house catered to black professionals, mostly teachers, who took the train to Rectortown, and were then taken by buggy to Willisville. The hostelry closed in the late teens.

The Gaskins family was dominant in Willisville during the 20th century's first half. William Gaskins, a butler at Welbourne, also had a shoe repair shop in the recent Bishop Howard III home opposite the church. His son, Richard Gaskins, "Papa Dick," to all, was a well-known landscape gardener, and his son, Richard Gaskins Jr., was Edith Sands' butler at Benton and cooked at Foxcroft. Richard Jr.'s brother, John Gaskins, was also a landscape gardener, mainly for the Colin McClouds of Upperville. For more than 35 years, Lucius Gaskins cooked for Mary Neville of Pelham.

Rose Gaskins, "Ma Rose," wife of William Gaskins, was the mid-wife, and her helper, in a sense the area pharmacist, was Chrissie Brewer, a former slave who had a herb or balm for every ache and hurt. They kept the community healthy. Chrissie once went up to Elizabeth Dulany Lemmon at Welbourne and said about the influx of Northerners, "Time was when you fit 'em," meaning fought them, "Now you let 'em in and sit down with 'em." She couldn't fathom that. Whenever one of the old masters or their offspring would ride by, Chrissie would say "Savant, Miss," meaning "Your servant, Miss." And one cannot forget Frank Henderson, Colonel Richard Henry Dulany's groom. He was a man so conscientious that he would shake snow off the box bushes.

PHOTO COURTESY *COURAGE, MY SOUL*

The 1924 Willisville Chapel

In 1923, Mary Dulany Neville of Pelham told Willisville churchgoers that if they could raise $1,000 toward the building of a new church, she would donate the remainder. Born in Paris, France, Mrs. Dulany was an artist, and she took it upon herself to design the church by drawing a picture of the future building, modeled very much like a French country chapel. Trustees Frank Henderson, Moses Peterson,

William Gaskins, Dudley Gaskins, and Daniel Hampton spearheaded a drive that raised the $1,000. Thomas Atkinson, a gentleman farmer from the Richmond area, and a relation to Mrs. Neville, selected the site on Mrs. Neville's land. John Allison put the building together, and Albert Hall and James Jackson added the notable stonework.

In total the bill came to $6,500—a record price for a black church in the Virginia Piedmont. Mary Neville contributed $5,500, with a small assist from Welbourne's Fanny Dulany Lemmon. Eva Gault Neville donated the Bible, Dudley Gaskins the communion set, Anna Gaskins the organ, and Moses Peterson the rug. The church bears the datestone, "Willisville Chapel 1924 June 29."

After the second room was added to the Willisville School in 1933, Anna Gaskins became principal and taught grades four through seven. Teaching the lower four grades were Flossie Furr, Jeanne W. Mallory and from 1938 through 1944 that talented musician, Mildred Boyde, who supplemented her teacher's salary by giving piano lessons for 50 cents a half hour.

Miss Boyde came from Waterford, where her children had won the first choral concert for black children's schools held at Leesburg's Providence Baptist Church. After Miss Boyde and Willisville won the 1938 cup, Waterford's Edna Coates sidled up to Miss Boyde and said, "You can come to Waterford any time you want, but be sure to leave when the sun goes down." For seven straight years, Miss Boyde and Willisville won the cup, and they retired the trophy. Today it rests in the Willisville Chapel.

After Anna Gaskins retired in 1950, Emma Olds, Louise V. Jones, and Louise Jones taught. Ethel Smith Stewart, teaching grades four through seven, and Edna L. Brinkley, handling the primary grades, closed the school's doors in June of 1963. Area children then went to Banneker Elementary in St. Louis.

Macsville

Where The Odd Fellows 'Turned Out'

With a population pushing 50, Macsville is one of Loudoun's larger villages, nearly twice the size of such nearby and better known neighbors as Dover, Mountville, and Pot House. Since 1900 this straggle of houses along Route 50, a mile and a half east of Middleburg, has been in print only once; on the post office map of Loudoun published about 1915, where it was spelled 'Macksville.'

A reason for its omission might have hinged on its being largely a Negro community, its small but neat bungalow-style homes being the successors of mean slave dwellings and outbuildings owned by the McVeigh family.

The McVeighs first settled in Loudoun in 1793. According to Norman McVeigh, his grandfather, Dr. James Harvey McVeigh, coined the name Macsville some two decades before the Civil War. The McVeighs were Philadelphians and back in the very early 1700s Jeremiah McVeigh married Mary Potts. They had a son, Jonathan, who lived in or near Philadelphia. Jonathan's son Jesse, born in Pennsylvania in 1770, was the first to settle in Loudoun, buying one of the original Middleburg lots from Leven Powell in 1793.

Jesse McVeigh apparently was a trader in grain, for in 1799 he leased an undisclosed amount of acreage from James Monteith of Stafford County. Yearly, his rent was a "full Quantity of thirty Bushels of Merchantible wheat delivered in the most convenient Merchant Mill." This was equivalent of $30 to $50 in today's value. The only hint at location, other than being in Loudoun County, was that the leasehold was "near Russells Meadow." Jesse added to his holdings on April 1, 1801, when he bought 185 acres for £262, 10 shillings (about $874) from the Skillman family. The buyer was described as "of the town of Middleburg," and again there was no hint of location other than it was part of "Cocks Patten," meaning an original patent or grant to Catesby Cocke from Thomas, sixth Lord Fairfax.

On December 12, 1805, Jesse McVeigh bought a second large parcel, 368 acres for $752.50 from John Bayly. Once more there is no description of the purchase, save for it being "part of [the Reverend Charles] Green's patent."

Putting these parcels together we see that today they straddle Route 50 in and around Macsville. Of interest, no mention is ever made of the old Ashby's Gap Road (Route 50), indicating that the tolls added in 1785 to improve the road's upkeep never amounted to much. Old deeds would generally play up a road through property, citing it as the "main" or "great road" from somewhere to somewhere, even if that were not the case. Only an 1806 survey of lands of "Russell & Bayly" shows the old road, but does not name it.

Jesse was not the only Loudoun McVeigh of the day. Jeremiah and wife Sarah, and Jonathan–who possibly were brothers of Jesse–owned land in Aldie and on Goose Creek. Their names, however, disappeared from deed books after 1804. Jeremiah and Sarah's last sale, on March 17 that year, noted that the land begins "at a white Oak Commonly Called the Navel Corner."

Jesse McVeigh and his wife Elizabeth had 14 children—14 who lived by the time he entered his will in 1833. He indeed was not in ill health at the time (he died in 1856), but was a careful and generous provider, indicating that 40 years in Loudoun had brought prosperity through wheat. Each child received either a substantial acreage or a minimum of $108 (equivalent to about $5,000 today), with most receiving $318 and a slave. His eight "youngest children" are noted as Nancy H. Rogers, Angelina, Frances Elizabeth, Amanda, Jesse H., Jonathan Milton, Benjamin Franklin, and Hannah Virginia. His elder set are Eli, the first son, Hiram, Townshend, James Harvey, William Newton, and Mary Ann Gibson.

Wills of that day served more than a legal purpose. In many cases they were the testaments of a lifetime, set forth in the introductions. Jesse McVeigh's will began: "Knowing the uncertainty of life, and truly aware that it is appointed for all men to die and after Death to come to Judgment and in full hopes at the grate Day of the General Reseraction [sic]to receive the Crown of glory pronounced from the beginning of the world and In hope of free Pardon of all my sins, and a Blessed Immortality freely and willingly resigning my precious soul to that God who gave it to me in full hope for the sake of Jesus Christ to receive free pardon of all my sins. And as for the worlds good as it had pleased God to bless me with I give and bequeath in the following manner to wit: Amen."

There were two McVeigh plantations when third son James Harvey gave the name Macsville to the slave dwellings, outbuildings, and warehouses that stood by the Ashby's Gap Turnpike. Both manor houses stand tall today: brick Mount Airy north of the pike, stone Valley View south of the pike. Both stand on land granted to the Reverend Charles Green in 1741. Since 1987, Valley View has been home to Wayne and Juanita Swedenburg's winery. When they began the operation Juanita told me that "what she really wanted to do was to market a good two-dollar bottle of wine."

Valley View plantation, now Swedenburg Vineyard PHOTO COURTESY LOUDOUN COUNTY DEPT. OF ECON. DEV.

Through a succession of partial inheritances, Mount Airy passed out of the McVeigh family on Aug. 30, 1904, when Richard L. Rogers bought the last share from Jesse P. McVeigh. Valley View left the family on January 2, 1911, when Milton M. Pearson bought the 300 acres from Sallie A., Jane E., Columbia, and Georgia A. McVeigh for $10,000. And wouldn't you know it, Milton's nickname was Mac, so the Macsville name continued.

Macsville changed slowly during those years. Every once in a while an old slave quarters or outbuilding would fall in, and a new bungalow arise in its stead. The one village business was Clarendon Fisher's shoe shop, a fixture of the 1920s through the forties.

Macsville was still a predominantly Negro community and beginning in the early twenties, in a field owned by Will Hall, each Memorial Day, Fourth of July, and first Friday in September—the Odd Fellows' "Turn Out Day"—blacks from near and far would pay fifty cents to see baseball, horse-racing, and marching bands from Washington. Another fifty cents would buy a fine barbecue. The day's festivities started with an early-morning gathering at the Federal Street Odd Fellows' Lodge in Middleburg. Then they would march down Washington Street to The Plains Road, back to the lodge, and then motor to Hall's Park. The Aberdeen Odd Fellows and its women's auxiliary, the O. L. Grant Lodge, the R. P. Dawson Elks Lodge, and Solon Cemetery trustees often sponsored the events, with proceeds going to Negro churches and schools, and for college scholarships. Five to six hundred persons attended the gatherings during their 1930s heyday, but with the gas shortage, new interests after World War II, and the $1.50 admission charge, the last Hall's Park galas took place about 1948.

Just west of the park, Melvin Amor Warren and his wife, Agnes Riddle Warren from Pittsylvania County, opened their six-room Stoneleigh Guest House in October 1939. They first catered to Florida-bound motorists, charging a dollar a night, double that if one stayed for the chicken dinner and breakfast—most did. After the eastward shift of Route 15 in 1941, race-goers and horse-showers were frequent guests. Stoneleigh stayed open through 1971. Mr. Warren, a talented wood-carver, taught art at Hill School and Middleburg Elementary, and also carried the Route Two mail—the St. Louis-Unison route—for 36 years until his 1961 retirement. He then drove a school bus for nine years.

Most folk, especially with a bent toward sports, now know Macsville for its Mickey Gordon Park, successor to Hall's Park. Mr. Gordon, a near-20-year member of the county's parks and recreation advisory board, was also a founder of the county's Babe Ruth Leagues. And, for others who just drive by, the highway department has added its contribution—a "Macsville" sign at each end of the village.

Howardsville

Home Of The Howards And Summerses

Jacob Howard came from Kentucky where he belonged to the Lawsons. Then he was sold to the Carters of Upperville. There he met Sophie who belonged to the Gochnauers–later residents of Loudoun than the Carters, who, in the person of Landon and George had received area grants of more than 16,000 acres back in 1731. Yet, on the eve of the Civil War, the Gochnauers had made their mark. Jacob Howard–Jake he was called–farmed for the Carters and sometimes drove the master's carriage. Sophie worked in Gochnauer homes.

By the end of the Civil War, or perhaps sometime later, Jacob and Sophie Howard moved to Grayson land three miles north. George M. Grayson had been a wealthy landowner of the area of Bloomfield and Union. The latter village officially became Unison in 1829, but Federalist politics aside, everybody still called it Union.

George Grayson died in 1850, and his will of November 20 left a large estate that included 28 slaves, valued at $6,980. Seventeen had names, if only first ones: Barney, Benjamin, Charity, Chilton, Edmunds, Eliza, Ginny, Hannah, Harriet, Harry, James, Maria, Mary Nelson, Scytha, Susan, Thomas–first settlers of Howardsville of some two generations later.

Disputes among the Grayson heirs led the Loudoun court to order Asa Jackson to survey Newstead, as the Grayson farm was called, with the survey of August 23, 1860, dividing the farm into three tracts: Belmont, 348 acres; Greenway, 238 acres; and the "Burnt House" tract, 145 acres. Next year, on June 19, William and Mary Stephenson bought the "Burnt House Wood Lot," 28 acres and the home of many Grayson slaves. A small lick of Piney Branch brought water for cooking and cleaning. The Stephensons paid $1,149 for the land that was to become Howardsville. It's not clear whether Grayson's former slaves were living on the Burnt House Wood Lot tract after the war; none of the first names of the former slaves match those of the first Howardsville landowners.

Black landholders first appear on December 12, 1874, when the Stephensons, for a price left blank in the deed, sold four acres to Jacob Howard and Andrew Causberry (Cosberry in later deeds). The same day they sold two acres to Jerry Basil for $50. All were farmers. Howard began laying stone walls, a specialty few former slaves were fond of. Sometime between the end of the Civil War and 1876, the Summers family, which formerly belonged to the Upperville Gibsons, heard about vacant land at the Burnt House Wood Lot, and moved there.

That November 4 the Stephensons sold another tract, one acre on the "road leading from Worrel's store to Bloomfield," to Armistead Summers for $45. And on March 29, 1879, the Stephensons sold two more tracts, two acres to the four remaining Summers brothers "Frank Summers & his Brothers Walker, Eli, & Clinton Summers," for $85. The same day another one-acre lot was sold to Jacob Colbert for $50.

Of the area in those early days AllinTibbs, born January 15, 1871, remembered Howardsville.

> "Howards were colored people. Was very few of them. I believe they was all Howards. Farmers, made baskets, rugs, shoemakers. The older ones, they was disabled, they made baskets, the younger ones got out and worked. Clarence Howard, Ben Howard, all an old mess of Howards. Jim Howard. I suppose they was slaves before the war."

Clarence and Jim were of the St. Louis Howards, another family. No one remembers Ben. "Old Man" Jake Howard had seven or eight children. We know of at least six: Evan, Letitia, Matilda, Mary, Peyton and Jake Green.

Late in life Old Man Jake was still laying stone fences, his last at Newstead, for its owner, Henry Frazier. It was about 1910; there was a section he never finished, and it is still unfinished. Helping him before he died was his grandson, Bishop Howard Sr., a little boy standing on tip-toe to hand his grandfather the rocks. Like his son, Bishop Howard Jr., whose family is still in the stone-laying trade, Bishop Sr. began by mixing the mud in gallon buckets. And, as he noticed how his grandfather carefully eyed each stone in the pile, and then fitted it in place, he got the knack.

Throughout his last forty years, "Uncle" Walker Summers made brooms, baskets, and repaired chairs. At the turn of the 19th century and before, they'd plant broom corn around the edges of the cornfields, as they often plant sweet corn today. When the broom corn ripened, they'd cut it off, season it, and then rip the top seed off. The corn husks did the sweeping. When the broom corn ran out, Uncle Walker would mend slit-bottom chairs with white oak saplings and would make clothes baskets and dog beds out of hickory splits. Uncle Walker died in 1930; the other Summerses are gone now.

A remembered lady about Howardsville–and nearly the whole of Loudoun's southwest corner–was midwife Amanda Basil. During the post-Civil War years and the early 20th century she brought numerous children, black and white, into the world. And at the same time she and her husband Willis raised eight of their own. Like most area black men, Willis worked about various farms, taking on any task.

PHOTO COURTESY THOMAS BALCH LIBRARY

One of the Howards' homeplaces

Before 1920, Howardsville children attended school at the schoolhouse at Rock Hill, more than two miles north. Rock Hill also had a tough reputation in those days. Better, some said, to keep the kids home. In those times Virginia law didn't require you to go to school if you had to walk more than two miles one way.

The same rule held when Howardsville children switched to the new Willisville School in 1919. That school was even farther from Howardsville—nearly three miles—though many cut through the Piney Branch bottom land between the Greengarden and Willisville Roads. Alberta Reid, granddaughter of Amanda Basil, told me that Howardsville children "wouldn't have even thought of not walking the three miles to school."

Nine homes, five of them dating from the days of early post-slavery, make up today's Howardsville. Nine houses and about 50 persons, many of them descending from the first families—Howards, Basils, Summerses. The triangle of woods speckled with houses would look much the same to Jacob Howard, even to the several-hundred-acre Piney Swamp, the village's vast borderland to the west. Only the road looks different, called by various names—Greengarden, Fletcher's, and Howardsville—and paved in 1963.

The Washington Post reporter Victoria Benning wrote a touching postscript to the village in 1996. Quoting Eli Summers's grandson, Thomas Reid Jr.: "I remember when you could stand on your porch and hear a car coming a quarter mile away and tell who it was by the time of the day and the sound it made."

Welbourne

Dulanys And More Dulanys

Five place names in Loudoun bear the designation "Welbourne." In order of age there is decaying Old Welbourne, once called Welbourne; the manor Welbourne, once called Welbourne Hall; the manor Old Welbourne, a replacement for the derelict Old Welbourne; the old post office and a trio of buildings that comprise the village of Welbourne; and the lane by the village, formerly called Welbourne Road.

The name is Old English; the "Wel" meaning "well" or a spring of water, and the "bourne" meaning either a boundary or destination point, or a brook.

For generations the Welbournes of Loudoun have been linked to the Dulany family, whose forbearers were the O'Dulaneys, medieval Irish from Queen's County. Daniel Dulany arrived from Ireland at Port Tobacco, Maryland, about 1703, and his second wife Rebecca Smith bore him a son, Daniel, in 1722.

The second Daniel Dulany was a noted lawyer who upheld in print the right of the colonists not to be taxed without representation in the English Parliament. But he was not sympathetic to the Revolution, and at its beginning retired to his home, Hunting Ridge, near Baltimore. During a brief visit to England in 1781, nearly all of his property was confiscated and thus his son moved to Virginia. The name Dulany's Valley now honors the family's Maryland tenure.

Benjamin Dulany, son of the second Daniel Dulany, married Elizabeth "Betsy" French, daughter of Daniel French, of Rose Hill, Alexandria, and the builder of brick Pohick Church in 1767. And through Daniel French's father, came the family's connection with Loudoun County; the elder Daniel French had bought land on Wankopin Branch in the 1740s.

On May 20, 1811, Benjamin and Elizabeth French Dulany gave 500 of their 2,000 Loudoun acres to sons John Peyton Dulany and Daniel French Dulany, and by agreement in 1815, John Peyton Dulany received 292 acres and about that time moved to Loudoun from Clermont, the family home in Fairfax County. Mr. Dulany and his wife, the former Mary Ann DeButts, lived at the now broken-down stone-and-log home known as Old Welbourne. In their day the house was called Welbourne or possibly Welbourne Hall, for in 1783, Mary Ann DeButts was born at Welbourne Hall in Lincolnshire, England.

Sometime during the 1820=1840 years, the original Loudoun Welbourne or Welbourne Hall became uninhabitable, most likely by fire. John Peyton Dulany's first thought was to build a new home on the ridge west of present Welbourne, but with four children, and two elderly female cousins who urged him to remodel an older home, he chose the latter course and moved to a late-eighteenth-century stone home, the present Welbourne.

As was the fashion of the period he had the building plastered in the Greek Revival style, and being a man of means he added wings to it about 1840. Sometime in the 1850s, the two-story front portico was added. The date "1836" appears in nursemaid Elizabeth Dulany Herbert's room.

Little-changed Welbourne, circa 1970 PHOTO COURTESY THOMAS BALCH LIBRARY

The original Welbourne of John and Mary Anne Dulany was not renovated until after 1852, and sometime later a new brick home arose close-by, built for Methodist minister Stephen Samuel Roszel, who had married Julia P. Dulany. Since father John P. Dulany called his renovated home, Welbourne Hall, the Roszel place became Old Welbourne. In time the renovated stone and log house became known as the "first" Old Welbourne.

John Peyton Dulany's son, Richard Henry Dulany, was a sportsman. About 1840, he founded the Piedmont Hunt, and, in the 1850s, started what is now the Upperville Horse Show. According to family tradition, the horse show began in 1853, after Richard noticed that farmers weren't treating their mares properly when in foal. He offered a silver cup to the farmer with the best colt, and when he went to see Jeweler Louis Tiffany in New York, Tiffany recognized a new potential for silver, donated the first cup and presented it to the winner. The *Southern Planter* notes the show as a reality in 1857.

The Civil War brought the Dulanys and cousins to secluded present Welbourne, a mile and a half from the main traveled Ashby's Gap Turnpike. John P. Dulaney was 76 years old at the war's outbreak, but son Richard enlisted, became a colonel in the 7th Virginia Cavalry, the Laurel Brigade, and near Lexington was shot in the right arm. He refused anesthesia because he was afraid the doctors would amputate the arm. They removed Richard's bone from elbow to shoulder. Later he learned to drive a dray four-in-hand. After the war the Upperville Horse Show never needed a policeman; the mere sight of Colonel Dulany's withered arm and sound of his strident speech was enough to stop a fight. His voice could control a horse.

One Welbourne Hall resident was Mr. Wiedmeyer, a Swiss schoolmaster who taught the Dulany children in a schoolhouse in front of the home. During the severe early November 1862 actions near Upperville, General J. E. B. Stuart's forces unsuccessfully contested the westward Federal advance on the hill west of the mansion. And when Union forces captured the grounds, they threatened to burn the home. Mr. Wiedmeyer intervened, exclaiming he was a Swiss citizen, that this was his home, and that there would be severe repercussions abroad should there be depredations. The officers heeded the warning.

As a reminder of a Confederate who stayed at the home, a window pane bears the cut "Lieutenant G. C. Walker October 28 62." The inscription was purportedly incised by "The Gallant" Major John Pelham, who was about to add his own name when he had to return to his artillery. Major Pelham's batteries stood on the hill west of Welbourne. An 1877 home there honors his name.

During the War of 1898 (the Spanish-American War), when a Colonel Frelinghuysen from New Jersey came down to Welbourne to buy horses for the conflict, he, without warning, asked Mrs. Richard Henry (Rebecca) Dulany how she felt when she saw blue uniforms in the front yard. "You really want to know?" she asked. "I felt like hiding the silver." And during the war the family silver was hidden in a grave originally intended for a slave child at Old Welbourne. After the Civil War they had a good deal of trouble finding where it had been buried.

The Dulanys had a chapel for their slaves built in the early 1850s. During the war the marauding Yankees turned it into a stable, and so it remained, a workhorse barn until 1922, when it needed either to be torn down or fixed up. The latter course was chosen, and Bluemont's John Kelley remodeled the building into a house, the residence of Elizabeth H. Lemmon, a granddaughter of Richard Henry Dulany. For many years she was remembered among literati for her long-time correspondence with writer F. Scott Fitzgerald.

During the 1920s, Elizabeth Lemmon's mother, Fanny Allison Carter Dulany Lemmon was the mistress of Welbourne Hall (since the turn of the century known as Welbourne). She and her husband, John Southgate Lemmon, ordered an automobile from R. Chamblin Steele, the Purcellville Ford dealer. Cham, thinking the Lemmons wanted only the finest, brought down a Lincoln. But when the Lemmons saw the name, they had the motor car returned. John had been a 17-year-old dispatch carrier for the Confederacy in 1861. On one of his missions, he swam across the Potomac near Leesburg.

John Peyton Dulany's will of 1873 indicated he had become one of Loudoun's wealthiest men. His two living children received $50,000; Richard Henry Dulany, a grand-son, received two-fifths of that amount and Mary A. Whiting the remainder. The will, however, noted that much of the bequest— equivalent to more than two million dollars today — was in stocks and bonds. The older Dulany died at the age of 93 in 1878, and it was after his death that the family graveyard just southeast of the oldest of the Old Welbournes was formalized with a fine fieldstone wall capped with limestone, a copper gate, and interior hemlocks to shade the tombstones.

In the graveyard rest numerous Dulanys, along with many families who intermarried with the Dulany family: Carlyle, Fairfax, Lemmon, McElhone, Morison, Neville, Randolph, Roszel, Smallwood, and Whiting. The stones of Richard Henry Dulany and wife Rebecca, Elizabeth Dulany Herbert, Henry Grafton Dulany, and Robert Neville and wife Mary Dulany Neville are tall crosses, indicative of their High Church Anglican heritage.

The Dulanys contributed heavily to Democrat Grover Cleveland's presidential campaign, and on May 7, 1886, the donations bore fruition in the form of a post office named Welbourne, in the midst of the many Dulany properties. James W. Iden became postmaster, followed by John T. Miley in 1887 and Pauline DeButts in 1900. Richard Henry Dulany paid a man to meet the train in Rectortown and buggy the mail to the Welbourne Post Office. These time-honored trips gave rise to the rumor that the boarding house by the railroad at Rectortown Station was known as the Dulany Club. John Peyton DeButts, Pauline's husband, was usually at the post office during her tenure, through June 29, 1907.

That date marked the end of the Welbourne Post Office, a scant year after the imperious Richard Henry Dulany's death at age 86. But the post office was not discontinued because of that event. A cousin, Robert Neville from Ireland, was exclaiming at the University Club in Washington about Welbourne Post Office, established at the whim of a man. This could never have happened in Ireland, said Neville. The man he was talking to happened to be a high official in Republican Teddy Roosevelt's administration, and in line with Teddy's policy of Rural Free Delivery, the Welbourne Post Office became a memory, and the RFD wagon from Middleburg took over.

During the 1920s there was a store at the old post office. It was operated for three or four years by "Old Man" George Kelley, and by someone no longer remembered for a year or two before. Just north of the old post office, Will Warner, of the Willisville Warners, ran a fine blacksmith shop, taken over by Thomas Lee Sacra in the teens. From 1921 until his death in the late forties, William "Bill" Smith ran the shop. The Welbourne post office still stands, the shop is gone.

Another R. H. Dulany business was the mill at Millville, locally pronounced "Millsville." The Chinn family ran this mill during Revolutionary times, and the community was a thriving one in pre-Civil War times. In postwar years Unison-area miller John F. Newton ran the manufactory. Then in the spring of 1892 high-speed rollers replaced the old machinery, and Bloomfield's William Mays became miller until the Millville Mill closed, about 1918. The mill was tall and frame, with a stone foundation. It probably had been rebuilt to replace a stone or brick structure destroyed during the war. One day Mr. Mays's turbine generator stalled—full of eels. For two days the mill sold fresh eel.

During Prohibition Harry Neville ran a still at the mill, well hidden in the basement, accessible only by a trap door. It wasn't discovered until someone noticed a new pipe going into the wall, uncovered, perhaps, by a small animal. The mill fell in with the flood of 1936.

A fixture near Welbourne from about 1918 until 1932 was the polo field at "Miss Lemmon's Bottom" along Goose Creek. William P. "Pappy" Hulbert and his Middleburg Polo Team first rode here because it was the only accessible flat ground between Middleburg and Upperville. In 1932 the team began playing at John S. Phipps' bottom, soon called Phipps' Field.

The Dulany legacy lives on at Welbourne PHOTO COURTESY THOMAS BALCH LIBRARY

Dr. Archibald Cary Randolph, of the Carter Hall Randolphs, Millwood, Clarke County, left two place names on the Dulany landscape. He had married Eva Randolph "Terry" Dulany, and was persuaded by her father, Richard Hunter "Dick" Dulany of Grafton, son of the imperious colonel, to retire at an early age at Old Welbourne. Dr. Randolph had been a prominent Charlottesville urologist. Terry then died young, as had the husband of her sister Rebecca "Cuppie" Dulany. So Dr. Randolph then married "Cuppie," the former Mrs. Fred McElhone. They're all together now, at the Old Welbourne graveyard. While Dr. Randolph lived at Old Welbourne a scant 17 years, the corner of the road by the farm today is called Randolph's Corner, and the lane leading west, Randolph's Lane.

Old-timers remember Dr. Randolph for his riding prowess on election day. They say he'd first cast a ballot at Welbourne, then Upperville, then Atoka, then Rectortown. Since he was prominent, and a newcomer, nobody quite knew to which Dulany home he was attached.

At present Welbourne manor, Frances "Fannie" Morison began taking in paying guests with proper introductions in the mid-thirties. She charged eight dollars a couple, including breakfast—the forerunner of the area bed-and-breakfast craze of the 1980s. If her prices were double those of Stoneleigh, the latter did not have the austere gazes of Colonel Richard Henry Dulany and Charles Willson Peale's Captain John deButts in the parlor entry. Son Nathaniel Holmes Morison Jr., and wife Sarah 'Sally' Harris, daughter of Stokes's Floyd Harris, continued the regimen in 1956—$70 a night for two—and their son, Nathaniel Holmes Morison III, and wife Sherry Weymouth Morison, took over in the early 1980s. Rates today are commensurate with its aura, and include a big Southern breakfast.

So much for Welbourne lore, but an aficionado might seek out the book *Memoirs of a Poor Relation* by Marietta Minnegerode Andrews and *The A. B. C. Book of Alexander Brown Chapman*. The search will not be easy, though; in the last few years both the Thomas Balch and Library of Congress copies have been "missing from shelf," and the *A. B. C. Book* was never sent to the Library of Congress. Miss Fanny Lemmon told me that the Minnegerode family tried to destroy all copies because of some "unflattering portrayals" of members.

Marble Quarry

Its Stone, Pride of The U. S.

The cluster of old frame buildings known as Marble Quarry struck its beginnings sometime before 1773, when Simon Triplett had a grist mill on the right bank of Goose Creek. The mill was located just across from today's Marble Quarry settlement, some three miles west of Oatlands and two miles east of Mountville on the Lime Kiln Road.

The Loudoun Court ordered surveyors on October 11, 1773, to lay out a "Road to begin near the Church and to lead to Simon Triplett's Mill." The church was the old Mountain Chapel, forerunner of Roszell Chapel. Before 1810 it stood in the corner of the Snickersville Pike and today's Jeb Stuart Road. That road laid out in 1773 is today's Lime Kiln Road.

On April 10, 1798, Simon Triplett and wife Martha sold their water, grist and saw mills on Goose Creek and 80 acres to Barnett Hough for £1000 (about $3,300). Just about that time, the Mount family, and later the Dodges and Will Carter, began to quarry three to four large limestone outcrops on both sides of the creek in the low lying hills which connect the Catoctin range with Bull Run Mountain. The lime was then crushed, burned, and sold to area farmers to sow on their tobacco-worn fields. Two restored lime kilns stand on the old Will Carter place, today's Wind Fields. Some more kiln ruins sit in the woods north of Lime Kiln Road, a mile or so west of Oatlands.

One of these quarries held more marble than limestone, and as the marble was of such fine quality, building contractors for the U. S. Capitol in the new "Federal City" gave the quarry a good hard look in the early 1790s. Problems of transporting the marble, however, led them to opt for the Potomac Marble of the Leesburg and Point of Rocks quarries.

Quarrying of lime lasted at least until the 1870s, with William F. Carter, owner of the operation. About that time, or perhaps a decade later, commercial lime and fertilizers closed down the operation.

Triplett's old mill, however, was still going strong. Barnett Hough and wife Louisa realized a 33 percent profit when they sold the same property to Daniel Brown of Frederick County, Virginia, on December 13, 1802. Brown ran into some hard times and in 1810 found himself in debt to John Lloyd of Washington for some $807. So that February 7th, Brown leased the mill to Fleet Smith and Thomas Gregg to pay off the debt. When Daniel and wife Rachel sold the mill to Jonathan Schofield on January 1, 1817, the 80-acre tract brought a tidy $12,500.

Either fire or flood had destroyed the mill, and on July 3, 1819, Jonathan and his wife Eleanor were forced to sell the same tract for $2,000 at public auction in Leesburg. The buyer was Richard Henderson, who a decade later was president of the Bank of Potomac in Winchester. The millers under Schofield and later under Henderson, when the mill was rebuilt, were James and Alexander Duer. When stock was sold in the old Goose Creek Canal, "Duer's Mill" was noted as one of the places stock could be purchased in 1832. Duer's Mill was to be a terminus of the canal.

Mr. Henderson sold the mill on January 22, 1836, to Jonathan Carter and the $1,200 purchase price might have mirrored the severe depression of the time rather than the mill's condition. Jonathan and his wife Elizabeth kept the mill until December 16, 1844, when it passed to John and Griffith E. Thomas in a trade. In the deed the property is cited as "a Merchant Mill known by the name of Franklin Mills," and the tract size 26 acres. Franklin was a traditional middle name of the Carter family.

In 1847, the Thomases sold the mill and five acres to William C. Palmer and James H. Silcott for $3,300, and in 1853 Silcott and Mason Chamblin passed the mill on to Burr P. Nichols for the same price. Two years later Nichols traded the mill to Samuel Millard of Fairfax County for 160 acres in Fairfax. In all these transactions the mill is cited in deeds as "Franklin Mill."

Then, on September 12, 1866, this interesting ad was inserted in the Leesburg newspaper, *Democratic Mirror* by Millard's miller, James R. Bowen:

> My mill known as the 'Yankee Mill,' one mile east of Mountville, is in good repair and I am grinding wheat and corn on old terms. I have also erected a distillery in the mill and am ready to furnish good Corn and Rye Whiskey in any quantity for $3 to $3.50 per gallon. I will also exchange whiskey for all kinds of products from a June apple to a bushel of corn.

So as not to offend area Quakers, Baptists, and Methodists in the same paper he placed another ad confirming that the distillery "does not, however, conflict with the interests of milling."

The name "Yankee Mill" came into use in the Civil War's latter days, when Federal troops ran the mill to supply corn and wheat to their hungry men and horses. But "Yankee" never held, and neither did Bowen's distillery, for when Millard sold to Mahlon Thomas, on December 23, 1868, the old name, "Franklin Mill" was on the deed. The selling price was $3,500 for the mill and five acres and no distillery was mentioned.

A year later, Benjamin Franklin Carter, who owned 400 acres surrounding the mill, agreed to open his lands for quarrying of marble. On March 30, 1870, the state legislature chartered the "Virginia Marble Company." Its officers were Mr. Carter, Burr Powell Noland, R. W. N. Noland, Job W. Angas, John W. Wright, Frederick P. Staunton, John D. Defreez, Jdm E. Lewis, Clinton Lloyd, and William E. Neolock–or at least that's the way the deed spelled some names. Ben Carter sold Virginia Marble the 400 acres for $26,666.66, which he received in company stock. The areas to be mined and for the "laying off a town or village" were leased for an additional $10 an acre per year. To grind the marble, company director Burr Noland bought the mill from Mahlon and Mary Thomas on December 23, 1870. The Thomases sold the property for $1,000 more than they had paid for it two years earlier.

Full-scale mining operations were scheduled to begin in 1875, and in anticipation, a work force of some 50 families, mostly former slaves, was brought in to work the quarries. They would live on the leased "town or village" lands.

To educate the workers' children, the Mercer School District bought a quarter acre from Eli H. and Elizabeth Nichols for $25 on January 7, 1874. In 1875 the frame Marble Quarry School was built. The building's stone basement survives, on the Lime Kiln Road described in the deed as the "road from Goose Creek Bridge to Middleburg." In 1896 the building became home of Zion Church.

PHOTO COURTESY DEBORAH LEE

The remains of an old home at Marble Quarry

Sometime before 1923, perhaps the previous year when school board records note the school as closed, Marble Quarry School moved two miles south to Sam Fred Road, in an area farmed by the prominent Negro farming family, the Berrymans. Father George had been a founder of the St. Louis Colored Colt Show, and his sons Raymond and Thomas, and daughter Amy, were hard workers, respected by all. At the new school, still named Marble Quarry, Gertrude Stewart taught from 1927-36, and Hazel Brown Madden from 1939-44. Besides teaching, Mrs. Madden gave children rides to school in her car. The school board paid her $1.50 extra a month for each child riding with her. She told me her monthly salary was then $65; white teachers got about $30 a month more. Charles Willis, who taught between the Stewart and Madden tenures, was Marble Quarry's last teacher, closing its door in the fall of 1946. The following spring children were bused to the new George Washington Carver School in Purcellville.

PHOTO COURTESY *COURAGE, MY SOUL*

New Zion Baptist Church

Marble Quarry School on Sam Fred Road became the New Zion Church in 1970, when a lack of potable water at the old Zion Church induced the congregation to move. By that time Marble Quarry village was in near complete decay and had been enhanced by hundreds of junk autos.

That was not the case decades before, when marble from the Virginia quarry was awarded medals at the 1893 St. Louis Columbian Exposition, the 1900 Chicago World's Fair, and the 1907 Jamestown Exposition. Within a few hour's drive today you can see the marble in the Confederate Memorials at Luray and Little Washington. According to Professor George P. Merrill of the U. S. Museum (today's Smithsonian), the marble "has the close compact texture, whiteness, and wax-like translucency so much sought by architects and artists, and found only in certain of the Italian and Grecian marbles."

Burr Noland owned the mill until its end, sometime before 1905.

In 1901 quarrying stopped for a time, until the Virginia Marble Company was reincorporated the following year. Thomas Carter, father of long time Leesburg miller Paul Carter, was miller in 1900 and 1901, and was followed by Thornton Brown who ran it as a saw mill for a year or two when he wasn't operating a threshing machine. By 1910 the mill was down, and gasoline operated crushers were pulverizing the stone.

When President Woodrow Wilson sounded the beginnings of the massive marble Federal buildings in Washington–architecture cited in the trade as "outer Mongolian Gothic–marble chips from the quarry, known to builders as terrazzo, were used in floors and walls. During these times and until about 1940, Cecil and John Connors ran the quarry under supervision of D. C. Sands.

With a moratorium on building during World War II, quarrying operations stopped, but in 1946 they resumed under ownership of Gustav Hertz. The terrazzo was used for laying of floors in New York and Boston commercial and apartment buildings. To insure continuous operation of the quarry, Hertz had William Altizer build a steel bridge across Goose Creek from the quarry to Lime Kiln Road. Previously, high water in the Goose had hindered shipping. Had there not been a bridge, the heavy trucks would have had a dickens of a time climbing the dirt Mountain Road south of the quarry. The new bridge cut the time to the Leesburg railroad depot by almost an hour.

At the quarry, test corings down to 90 feet showed presence of both green and white marble, and Mr. Hertz's contract called for shipping of both. His men, however, could never find much green marble, and that, plus continued pumping of water from the 60-foot-deep pit caused operations to finally cease in 1949. On the last day the pump at the Quarry bottom was seen half under water; next morning it was covered. There it remains, beneath greenish-blue Caribbean colored water that is opaque from its mineral content. Through the sixties the quarry pond was a favorite swimming hole.

Professor Merrill and other geologists felt that if the quarry were not within 300 feet of Goose Creek, the pit's ultimate depth would have produced stone that would have been the pride of the United States. If you could see the huge slabs that line the quarry walls you would believe it.

Brown's Corner

The Browns, Halls, And Kennedys

Most call it the outskirts of Middleburg. A few know it as Maryland, and some call it Brown's Corner—a huddle of four houses, their outbuildings, and a church a quarter mile east of Middleburg at the corner of the old Ashby's Gap Pike and Sam Fred Road.

The corner dates back to the early 1770s, at least, when Sam Fred Road, then a through travelway to Leesburg, wound up the Wankopin Branch valley to Thaddeus McCarty's grist mill. The mill was on Goose Creek at the old Middle or Mountain Road, now Snickersville Pike.

Brown's Corner acquired its name sometime after 1855, the year Edwin Conway Broun (pronounced Broon) bought land from Elizabeth J. Short a mile north of the corner. About 15 years later, at the corner, in the plastered stone cottage, lived Joseph and Sarah Brown, who probably took their surname from the Brouns, a prominent Middleburg family. Regarding Joseph and Sarah's roots, their grandson's wife, Georgia Brown wrote me in 1976:

> Both Joseph and Sarah were free Born, their mother's mothers having been given their freedom before Emancipation [1862]. Their progress fantastic, Especially in Virginia. Many Masters, who held their House Servants in high esteem and affection, freed the mothers of their children…we do know that Sarah was not born on the Broun estate, Sarah was a Miss Moten of Middleburg, free Born,…the Motens, highly Cultured, Educators,…Sarah and Joseph, reared and Educated Seven Children, Sons and Daughters,…They held dear Their Rich Heritage, they were Cultured, Talented, Courageous and excellent Citizens,…

From such stock, on August 4, 1896, Chauncy Depew Brown, endowed with the gift of music, was born at the Joe Brown Place. He was raised by his grandparents, Joseph and Sarah. One day about 1910, Chauncy's neighbor, builder Willie Hall, told Chauncy that he was going into Washington to buy him a guitar, and that day Chauncy waited all day by the pike until Willie returned with his first instrument.

The Halls were newcomers to the corner. Will Hall and his builder brother, Albert, were sons of Nathan Hall, who had moved here from Berryman's Lane. Nate had been a master stonemason and builder of the post-Civil War era. When his sons came of age in the early 20th century, they founded the firm W. N. Hall & Son, builders of such notable Middleburg stone public buildings as the Phoenix Building, old

Middleburg National Bank, Firehouse, and Upperville's Fauquier-Loudoun Bank (now the Upperville Post Office). The fame of this Negro firm spread, and in 1932 they were honored with the contract to rebuild George Washington's grist mill at Mt. Vernon. After World War II, as the largest building firm in Loudoun, they built the new wing of the Leesburg Hospital.

In 1914, Albert Hall remodeled and added onto his house at the northwest angle of Brown's Corner. In the concrete walk he etched the date and the words "Maryland Heights." As to the name's origin, the Hall family speculates that since they often entertained relatives from

Chauncey Brown's home, Brown's Corner

PHOTO COURTESY THOMAS BALCH LIBRARY

Washington and Pennsylvania, they may have given the gathering place a nickname. which sometimes took a third form, "Baltimore Corner."

By 1915 neighbor Chauncy Brown, who could play guitar, drums, saxophone, and violin, had organized a band. His band lasted some 60 years and was known by no name except that of its leader—a great musician who had the gift of bringing people together. "He had a beautiful life among people," his widow recalls.

Chauncy Brown married Georgia White of Warrenton in 1921, then moved to her home town. There he received his only formal musical training from Mrs. Brown's father, Joshua Wayne White, noted teacher of the bass violin. Mr. White was an accomplished player of all wind instruments, as well, and founder of the Warrenton Concert Band in the late 1880s.

Chauncy Brown was a byword in hundreds of homes in Loudoun and Fauquier. He became the Hunt Country's favorite musician after his appearances at J. Walter Chrysler's North Wales estate south of Warrenton, in the early 1930s. At Upperville's Buchanan Town Hall, his playing would coincide with Lester Lanin's Gold Cup appearances in Warrenton. Lester came off second best, because Chauncy always had the music for the occasion; at Upperville it was Old English hunting songs and ballads. Many remember his playing at the Christmas-time Leesburg Assembly Dances, held between World War I and II, first at the Opera House, then at the Thomas Balch Library. Chauncy would also play at the Thomas Balch summer subscription dances in the '30s, and was a smiling face to many young children at Middleburg Christmas concerts of the '50s and '60s.

Duke Ellington played in Chauncy's band during the early '20s, as did several members of the Duke's band into the late '30s. In his 1973 autobiography, Mr. Ellington noted that Chauncy

> "worked with us [as a drummer], and sometimes we worked with him—a case of one hand washing the other. He is the society musician right there in the middle of that society swirl…I wonder if I would have been that lucky if I had stayed in Washington?"

Three of Chauncy's stalwarts through the years were Robert Burke of Arlington, sax and accordion; Armond Cole of Washington, piano; and Doc Perry of Washington, piano. Chauncy usually played guitar, often strolling among the listeners and dancers, singing with his light baritone, or harmonizing in tenor voice. He was fond of all types of music—except rock and roll.

Leesburg's Janet Harrison remembered these familiar lyrics, styled and composed by Chauncy during the Depression years:

Oh I don't bother work
Work don't bother me
I'm just as happy as
A bum, bum bumblebee
I eat when I can get it
I sleep most all the time
I don't give a dog gone

If the sun don't ever shine
Oh I go every where
I don't pay no fare
'Cause I can hop a freight car
Most any ole where
That's why I'm happy as
A bum, bum, bumblebee
'Cause I don't bother work
And work don't bother me.

With the Browns gone, and then the Halls gone, the corner slumbered after World War II and until the late 1950s when Bettina Belmont Ward had the first structure built at the corner in a century or so. It was a stuccoed concrete-block kennel for her show dogs. In 1962 the building became the area's first animal hospital. In 1977, Dr. John B. Holland's Blue Ridge Veterinary Clinic became the Middleburg Animal Hospital.

By that time–1959 to be exact–Sam Fred Road had been paved from the corner to Featherbed Farm, about two miles north. Samuel H. Rogers Fred, whose Sunnybank Farm the pavement passed, wasn't too keen about it. Both he and his father, Samuel Rogers Fred, had been foxhunters, and pavement was hard on horses' hooves and the dogs' scents. Besides, they had seniority on the road–150 years between them. Nevertheless, paving won out, and the blacktop reached the Snickersville Pike in 1966.

Paving, however, would have come a few years later, when a few hundred yards north of the corner, a church arose. It was St. Stephen the Martyr Church, a pleasant brick sanctuary designed by Vienna, Virginia, architect, Martin Elliot. St Stephen's is sometimes dubbed "the church the secret service built."

In February 1961, President and Mrs. John F. Kennedy rented Glen Ora, south of Middleburg and began worshipping at Catholic services held at the Middleburg Community Center, celebrated by the Reverend Albert F. Pereira. Seven and one-half months later, John S. Pettibone donated 3.8 acres for a new church. Through the efforts of the Pettibones, Thomas Lynch, Harold J. Deering, and Harold D. and Adelaide W. Menken, funds were collected for a sanctuary.

For a new building they asked the well-heeled for $500, but when Father Pereira approached President Kennedy, he did not feel it proper to mention a specific amount. The President, getting to the point, said: "How much do you want to stick me for?" He was relieved that it was only $500, but Father Pereira then felt that if the exact amount were known, people would think the President stingy. A St. John's (Leesburg) parishioner privately processed the check.

The Secret Service specified that next to the Confessional there be a soundproof and bulletproof usher's room with a direct phone line to the White House. The large windows appear opaque from the outside, and the blue-and-gray color scheme–shades of the Civil War Centennial– enlivened bare cinder-block walls.

President Kennedy's Church in Washington was St. Stephen's–for the Biblical deacon and first Christian martyr of Acts 6:1-6, 7:5-6–but that name was not the congregation's first choice. They wanted "Our Lady of the Hunt," but Virginia Bishop John C. Russell said, "No." Then they picked "Saint Hubert," patron saint of hunters. Bishop Russell again said, "No"–he wanted a name anchored in the Bible. So St. Stephen the Martyr it became, with Bishop Russell consecrating the church on April 21, 1963. The 1885 vision of Father Thomas J. Wilson, who had prayed for "a neat Church in Middleburg," had been answered.

PHOTO BY JOHN EMIG, CIRCA 1975

St. Stephen the Martyr, consecrated 1963

The President attended six Masses at St. Stephen's, always sitting on the aisle, next to last pew on the right. The Secret Service filled the last pew. The last Mass he celebrated was November 10th 1963, twelve days before he was assassinated. Father Pereira's sermon for the 10th was to be "the effects of hatred in our country," but he changed the message to "what death should mean to a Christian.' The sermon offered the belief that "Christian death is a passing over, an exodus which begins at our baptism." The sermon ended with a paraphrase from the Apocalypse of John (Revelation 21:3-5): "Behold the dwelling…Behold, I make all things new."

In 1967, Mrs. Robert Wong, buyer of Wexford, the Kennedy home near Atoka, initiated the Loudoun-Fauquier John F. Kennedy Memorial Fund, through which money could be funneled to beautify the church and finish the interior. The congregation repainted the blue-gray color scheme in 1968, opting for Williamsburg gold, white trim, and red carpet. A summer, 1968, tour of the Kennedy buildings–Glen Ora, Wex - ford, and St.Stephen, raised funds to build the steeple the next year and the portico in 1970. The Paul Mellons of Upperville donated the dogwood and boxwood around the church and their horticulturists, Charles Pecora and Everett Hicks, donated their time and experience in landscaping. The bronze bell made in Holland was not added until 1974, and bears that date. Did it toll for the passing of Chauncy Brown on November 11 of that year?

Bowmantown

In The Flat Below The Hollow

Named for the Bowman family, their homeplace since at least 1840, the village south of Aldie is a collection of about 25 dwellings; an old and a new church, an old schoolhouse, and a store that closed in the late 1970s. The area's first black settlers were free Negroes in the early 1800s, and the oldest residents who can be traced are Jim and Frances Bowman, born here in the 1830s, and Frank Napper, a freed Negro from Alexandria, who migrated to this Bull Run Mountain country shortly before the Civil War. His son, James Napper, was 96 when I interviewed him in 1976.

Sometime before the Civil War, Jim and Frances built a still-standing log cabin, where their son, Frank Bowman was born in the early 1850s. Frank married Lauvenia (born1860) in the late 1870s, and they had three sons: James, Walter, and Berkeley, whose families all settled nearby, giving the area–broadly known thereabouts as "on the mountain" or Bull Run Mountain–the name Bowmantown, in common use since the early 20th century.

With difficult times after the war, prayer groups organized at various homes, solidifying in 1873 into the Mount Pleasant Baptist Church congregation. Quoting from the church's 1971 history:

> In the early 1870s, there wasn't any organized colored church in this neighborhood, but there were a few Christians beyond the middle age who had been baptized into various churches. These Christians, in part were Brother John Allen and wife, Sister Julia Haney, Nellie Eweny, Amanda Ramey, Nellie Jones and a few others. These few would meet from time to time and hold song and praise services. Their meetings were indeed spiritual.

Some of these residents had worshipped at the integrated Long Branch Baptist Church at Halfway, Fauquier County, six miles away and almost a two-hour ride across Bull Run Mountain. Long Branch had a long tradition of mixed worship. In 1833 its congregation numbered 128 whites and 112 blacks, and in 1861 its congregation numbered 137 whites and 101 blacks. One of the white Brothers at the venerable Long Branch (organized in 1786), John Thomas Edmonds, was ordained to become first minister to Mount Pleasant Church across the mountain. From 1873 to about 1882 he rode to his congregation every Sunday, and about 1875 oversaw the building of a log church on the east slope of Bull Run. Because of its situation overlooking the Bull Run valley, the church was named Mount Pleasant.

Under the leadership of Brother Samuel Peter Fisher, the congregation grew, and the second Mount Pleasant Church was built in 1887. The church history notes, "Some were willing, some predicted failure. But unmindful of predictions, amidst great rejoicing the work was brought to completion." Still standing on its stone foundation, with small open belfry perched on the entranceway, second Mount Pleasant bears the roughly lettered datestone, "Mt. Pt. B July 31 YR 1887." To the west and south of the church, on a steep hillside is the graveyard. Nearly all the headstones are hand-hewn and the inscriptions hand-carved. The cleared south section, landscaped with roses, lilies and iris, looks like a hillside rock garden. Bordering the garden on its north is a huge oak tree, site of the first log church.

PHOTO COURTESY *COURAGE, MY SOUL*

1887 2nd Mount Pleasant Baptist, Bomantown

By the early 1880s, a combined Bowmantown and Stewartown–

the former's sister village a half mile west–had more people than Aldie. But as very few post offices were placed in Negro communities, when the U. S. Post Office Department decided on an area post office, they put it a mile from each village, at a one-house location known in 1885, as Levy, named for storekeeper Harris Levy.

In 1891 a frame, one-room public schoolhouse was built about a quarter-mile north of the church on the New Mountain Road. This road was called "new" when it was cut through eleven years before as a replacement for the old Deep Hollow Road or Meetinghouse Lane that struck south from Aldie, a half-mile west. Bennie Allen, a neighbor to the school, was the teacher. Since 1883 he had been teaching youngsters at the church, which had doubled as a public school. The site of this school was at the northeast corner of the old lane leading from New Mountain Road to Bowmantown and the Carolina Road. The school first referred to in records as "School E," was then named Bull Run, for the mountain.

The mountain, in turn, was named for the stream, Bull Run, the north branch of Occoquan River. Bull Run first appears in records of the 1730s, probably named for early settler William Bull. Miss Maude Ewell, that mountain story-teller, however, recounted many years ago of how an errant bull, chased for miles along the stream's course, gave the run its name.

Before 1898 the school burned, so classes moved to the abandoned log church. Emory Turner, of Middleburg, taught there until the still-standing Bull Run School, 600 feet north of the old school, on the west side of New Mountain Road, was built in 1909. Cornelia Smith Lyons taught at the school from before 1923 until 1939. Bull Run closed in 1948, and children were bused 15 miles to Leesburg or 12 miles to St. Louis, nearly an hour's journey. Converted to a dwelling, today the frame school is painted red, true to the northern image of the Little Red Schoolhouse. Virginia schoolhouses bore a white color, as did the churches, which often stood by their side.

At Mount Pleasant Church, Brother Richard P. Dawson, who had become pastor of Middleburg's Shiloh Baptist in 1886, became pastor of Mount Pleasant in 1894 and served until 1923. The church history notes the lean, mustached cleric as a "pulpit orator, gifted in song and power in prayer." Brother Arthur Stewart received the call to the pastorate after Brother Dawson, and served until 1940.

Few white denominational churches today use the terms Brother and Sister, though these greetings were given to Brethren in most Baptist churches in the 19th century, and still hold among Primitive Baptists and other Biblically oriented Christian Churches. The greeting is expressed well in the Pilgrim Psalm 133: "Behold how good and how pleasant it is for brethren to dwell together in unity!"

The village's one store, Neal Corum's, is just one-tenth of a mile from New Mountain Road on the south side of the lane to the village. "Kid" Corum ran the store from 1931 until he became ill in 1977. He was a firm man, spoke what was on his mind, but had a compassionate heart. He and his wife, Ollie Mae, reared Roy Trammell from the time he was three months old. Roy's father had been killed and his mother had four other children. Roy, a former Loudoun Deputy Sheriff, credits the Corums for his being where he is today. John Douglass, miller at Aldie, would often recall how Mr. Corum and Charlie Willis, operator of the store at Levy, would come into the mill and pick up some flour for resale. When Charlie or Kid bought a few bags of meal, John would say, "Business a little slow? Why Kid, you just picked up 100 pounds."

In 1950, Brother Lawrence A. Jackson became shepherd of Mount Pleasant and saw need of a new church for a growing congregation. He started a building fund and each member was asked to give $100 a year. When Reverend Jackson left the congregation in 1965, more than $30,000 was in the fund. Many who gave never saw the completion of the church in 1971. It was built in a clearing on the old Carolina Road, just east of Bowmantown. The attractive brick church presents a cross-like appearance with its two wings on either side of the pulpit, and like the old Mount Pleasant datestone, its marker encapsulates the church's history and that of the nearby village: "Mt. Pleasant Baptist Church Organized 1873 Built 1887 Rebuilt 1971 Rev. E. E. Terry."

Levy

Harris, A Jew, And Charlie, A Black Man

It was spelled "Levy" and was pronounced "Levi"–a village founded by Harris Levy, some 3,000 years after the first Levi, son of Jacob, received 48 villages scattered through Canaan as his inheritance. But unlike the Levi of the Old Testament, there was no Moses to record Harris's journey.

When Harris Levy arrived in Leesburg is not certain. Some say he came as a sutler—a type of vendor who followed the Union armies in their conquest south—selling hard-to-get staples; coffee, sugar, for hard-to-pay prices. Others say he came right after the war, a large sack on his back, plying clothes, dry goods, and shoes to the folk who lived in the hills and hollows of Bull Run Mountain.

To many he made an impression. They had never seen a "real" Jewish person. If there were Jews in Loudoun County before Harris, they had not advertised the fact. But Harris carried his faith and heritage proudly. As he passed by Mount Zion Church he remembered that Zion was the City of David–his city as well. He knew the Baptists understood. Harris Levy laid his sack on the ground early in 1885, some two miles southwest of Mount Zion. In 20 years of backpacking in the mountains he still had not made enough to buy a piece of land. His customers were the mountain poor, they rarely made it down to Aldie, Haymarket, or Middleburg. Sometimes they paid cash, other times they fashioned Harris a cloth cloak or homemade vest of beaver skin.

The land where Levy built his store was located at the corner of what was then called the Carolina and Landmark Roads. A good location: Landmark Road took you up over the mountain Levy knew so well and into the wealthy Landmark country of Fauquier. At the corner, a gentleman by the name of Pearson ran a blacksmith shop, and a half-mile south on the Carolina Road, Joseph Taylor ran a small grist mill on Bull Run.

That January 5, 1885, Henry Akers sold less than an acre at this northwest corner to Elizabeth Simpson. The price was $20, and there was no building on the property until that spring, when Harris Levy put up a small frame store, with permission of Miss Simpson. In a few years, perhaps, he'd have enough money to buy the land, and maybe a little more for a house and field for a cow.

James A. Conner had helped Grover Cleveland to an easy victory in Loudoun over Republican James G. Blaine. So, as a small reward, Conner was offered the postmastership and profits of a new post office–should, of course, he wish to start one.

And why not in Harris Levy's store? Harris Levy was a popular man. So the latter-day village of Levy was born. Five years later, on November 21, 1890, Harris Levy purchased his two and one-half acres from Miss Simpson for $175. The property, at the corner of "the Caro-

Charlie Willis's store at Levy

PHOTO COURTESY THOMAS BALCH LIBRARY

lina and Landmark Roads," was described as "A store house and lot that he the said Levy now occupies." Now they may have spelled it that way, and Harris even wrote it that way, but everyone–including Harris pronounced it "Levi." That's how it was spelled on the first Loudoun postal RFD maps of about 1915, and the first Loudoun highway map of 1932.

Shortly after Harris bought his store, it burned to the ground. Just about a year before, the Little River congregation had dismantled their

1814 brick church, so Harris bought the brick, had it hauled over to his demolished store and rebuilt the building in brick. After the store burned, however, the post office moved south to what was known as the old Skinner Place, just a few hundred feet from Bull Run and the Prince William County line. There it stayed, still with the name Levy, through a succession of postmasters. Herman R. Smith, the last postmaster, closed its doors on January 15, 1906. With the closing, mails were carried by horseback over Bull Run Mountain by the Landmark Road and into The Plains. But soon Pearson's blacksmith shop closed, and as Taylor's Mill had stopped running a decade before, the rural route could no longer be justified. About 1910 The Plains RFD route to Levy was shifted into Aldie.

By this time Harris Levy had retired to Alexandria, and J. E. Flaherty ran the store. But Mr. Flaherty wanted to move to Ashburn, so on November 22, 1913, Harris Levy and his wife Esther, sold their two and one half acres, "improved by a brick store house, dwelling and other buildings" situated at "Levy," to Charles H. Willis.

As Levy hadn't had much money in 1885, Willis was just as short in 1913. No matter, Levy asked for a down payment of five dollars, with the remainder to be paid off in $50 installments every three months. On September 3, 1920, Charles Willis had fully paid his debt. He ran that store, known in later decades as "Charlie Willises at Levi Corner" until 1974. Even old Rodney Purcell in Purcellville couldn't claim running a store for 62 years.

Besides running the store, Willis taught at the black children's schools at Aldie, Watson, Marble Quarry, and Mountville. When he taught, his wife Rosa ran the business. The old brick store burned in 1964 but Willis built it back in brick and block. As you pass by on the old Carolina Road, you can still see brick of the 1814 Little River Church facing the store's new east side. Of the rest of old Levy's store, Jack Hutchison took the safe and used it for a stile until it rusted away.

Stewartown

Above The Flats, Up In The Hollow

Atop Bull Run Mountain, two miles directly south of Aldie, sits the village of Stewartown, or to use correct English, Stewart Town, ten or so homes, and the legacy of a few former-slaves who settled there in the late 1860s. The name did not appear on a map until 1972, and "Stewartown" may not have been coined until the 1930s, when the children of Charles Stewart were growing up.

Within five days, in January of 1868, members of the Tavenner family sold two properties to former slaves. On January 16, "Phillip Stewart (colored)," as the deed called him, bought 10 acres and a right-of-way from "the mountain road through the said Reserve Lot," for $400. On January 21, "John Barnes, colored," bought two adjacent acres for $200.

The "mountain road" is today's New Mountain Road, and the right of-way is the segment of the Buchannon Gap Road extending from the New Mountain Road into Stewartown. In those days the gap road was often called the Landmark Road because well into the next century it crossed Bull Run Mountain into the rich Landmark country of upper Fauquier. The fork where the road split used to be called Bentley's Corner, for William and Ann Bentley raised their several children in a house that stood in the present grove of locusts.

Philip Stewart and John Barnes were not the area's first settlers, though, possibly Benjamin Hagenman was. In 1814 he bought 51 acres from Charles F. and Frances Love and in 1817 he bought 21 acres from Charles Fenton Mercer. Through the 1820s, Hagenman bought and sold mountain land around Cool Spring in Fauquier and Loudoun.

Cool Spring is the name for the main head spring of Bull Run. There is a smaller spring, not named, a few hundred feet to the south. From Cool Spring the Prince William County boundary winds along Bull Run to the east. The Fauquier-Prince William County boundary follows the crest of Bull Run Mountain to the south. That boundary runs along an old top-of-the ridge travelway called Skinner's Road. There were Skinners all over the ridge. The Fauquier-Loudoun boundary bears west by a straight line.

When George Love surveyed that line in 1824, he noted that Ben Hagenman's spring house stood by Cool Spring and that his home stood 825 feet west of the spring, on the Loudoun side of the boundary. The home is not there today. Close-by the home, tumbling down to Hunger Run, was a small branch that Love or Hagenman named Cool Spring Branch. The branch, however, did not empty into Cool Spring–at least not above ground.

The land about Cool Spring did not become very populous until the 1880s. Erman Downs, who was raised in the Bull Run Mountain country at that time, recalled that the land was very stony and most men "had a little place of their own. Some of the men got a day's work where they could. They had enough cows and chickens, and cash to get out and buy a pair of shoes."

Cash and the stock often came from gathering sumac, for the red flowers were used as a dye, and dealers awaited shipment at The Plains railroad station. Alice Downs, Erman's aunt, raised a family of eight by selling sumac and lived up in the mountain right after the Civil War.

Alice wasn't a church-goer, but nobody in her family went to bed until she read something from the Bible. She might have gone to Long Branch Baptist at Halfway a couple of times a year, but as Erman says, "she lived Christianity." In the Bull Run Mountains, "they just lived. They were not activists. They just took life as it comes and enjoyed it."

Several in the mountains remember the story of the mountaineer who got a lift aboard a wagon headed for Washington, a city he had never seen. The wagon stopped for the evening at Bailey's Crossroads, and the mountaineer got out in the night and looked in all directions for the mountains. There was just flat earth and sky. He knew what direction he'd come from, and the next morning he was back at his mountain home. He had walked all night.

Among some of the black families settling near Cool Spring in the 1880s were Luther and Lizzie Stewart, who bought less than an acre for $56, and insured their home for $125 the same day it was purchased, August 26, 1889.

Then there was Norman Stewart, who on December 15, 1881, bought nine acres of flood plain for $5 from Cuthbert "Cut" Rogers. After the flood of 1889, Stewart had to sell it, and he moved to the Landmark country of Fauquier. Norman Preston Stewart and his wife,

Angeline "Annie" Bryant, are the known ancestors of today's clan of Stewarts. He came to Loudoun as a slave, with his father, Ashby Stewart.

Just west of Stewartown, and 120 feet lower than the village, is Buchannon Gap, named for a family whose name has evolved from Buckhannon in the 1880s to Buchanan today. Most people in the mountains pronounce the name "Buckanan," but the family prefers "Byu-canan."

Sinah Buckhannon and Nancy Buckhannon bought 12 acres near the gap in 1833, each paying $400 for the land–a steep price to seller Hampton R. Brown. Two years later George and Frances Buckhannon bought land close-by, and in 1888 they sold their 11 acres to Luther and Frances Buckhannon. It was Luther for whom the gap was named, because he lived in a stone house by the pass. Luther, who worked for Henry Fairfax at Oak Hill, left Loudoun for Richmond in the 1920s.

In 1900 the following black families owned land described in property books as either "Near Levy" or East of Bull Run Mountain: Luther and Amy Buchanan; Zack Reed; Robert Peterson; Andrew and Martha Henderson; Harriett, John, Mary, and Wesley Allen; Ambrose, Warren, and Sol Corum; and Ed Fletcher. The Stewarts, absent from the 1900 property list, did not return to the mountain until 1927 when Charles "Uncle Charlie" Stewart, the son of Norman and Annie Stewart, came home.

Charles Stewart was talented. He bottomed and caned chairs, made baskets, dug ditches, and did a little bit of everything. During the summer he sharecropped. Most of the mountain Stewarts are among his issue: the Reverend James M. Stewart, pastor of Mount Pleasant Church, Ann Stewart Hatcher, Lizzie Stewart Harris, Lucinda Stewart Williams, Alfred Stewart, and Mary Stewart Whitener.

The village that by 1950 had taken Charles Stewart's name was generally referred to as "up in the hollow," to differentiate its location from the sister village of Bowmantown "down in the flats."

In recent years Stewartown and the Stewarts may well be remembered for producing one of the finest singing groups in the Virginia Piedmont. Elizabeth Stewart, wife of the Reverend James Stewart, started by forming the Stewart Singers of Mount Pleasant Baptist in the mid 1950s. By 1971 her son, James Stewart Jr., had started a junior choir. By 1976 that group had become the James Stewart Faith Gospel

Singers, a group of 20 musicians who specialized in gospel music and spirituals. Led by James Stewart Jr., piano, and accompanied by Ricardo Wright on the guitar and Wayne Trammell on the bass, the Faith Gospel Singers appeared in Washington, New York, and at the Bluemont Concert series.

The Faith Gospel singers are now a memory, but on Sundays their singing lives on at Mount Pleasant Church.

PHOTO COURTESY *COURAGE, MY SOUL.*

Mount Pleasant Baptist Church serves Stewartown and Bowmantown

Foxcroft School

Mens Sana In Corpore Sano

Mother, may I go out for a swim?
Oh, my darling daughter!
Hang your clothes on a hickory limb,
And don't go near the water!

This Old English nursery rhyme gives the title to "My Darling Daughter," the unpublished reminiscences of Rosalie Haxall Noland (1852-1935), mother of Charlotte Haxall Noland, founder in 1914 of one of our country's foremost schools for girls, Foxcroft, at the Pot House, Loudoun County. Mrs. Noland's recollections of her family were taken down on paper and tape and were then typed by daughter Rosalie Haxall Noland Ball in 1958-1959. Together, they present a shining account of Miss Charlotte's pre-Foxcroft years and of past life in the Middleburg area.

"Charlotte was born during the terrible blizzard of January-February, 1883. The doctor, Uncle William Cochran, could hardly make the trip from Middleburg to Burrland." Their home, Burrland, is a mile south of Middleburg, just over the line in Fauquier. It was built in 1880, the gift of Burr Powell Noland, father of Cuthbert Powell Noland, husband of Rosalie.

"I wrote to my mother in Richmond, telling her I was going to name the baby Octavia, after her. The letter took a week or so to get to Richmond, and my mother's answer took another week to reach me, and for these several weeks the child was known as Octavia. Then came the reply—she wished no child to be given such a name; she would not allow it. Instead, she said she greatly desired the child to be named Charlotte, after the daughter who married Robert E. Lee Jr., and then tragically died of tuberculosis just a year later. I was glad, indeed, to name the baby girl Charlotte, for I had greatly loved my beautiful sister and deeply mourned her death.

"Charlotte was never at a loss for an idea: she was full of energy and full of interests. She took the lead where groups were gathered. She named the game; she suggested plots for plays. She had to assert herself or go under. When any of the family was sick, Charlotte was in her element. To her, the entertainment offered to the patient was as important as the medicine. One night as she was saying her prayers, she sat back on her heels and asked: 'Why is God named Howard?' I asked her for particulars and suggested a mistake. 'Not at all, every morning we all say, Our Father, who art in heaven, Howard be thy name.' "

"I do not regret the lack of movies and radios during those years before the turn of the century. My children had to provide their own entertainment and had to develop their imagination. Their books and magazines were not numerous. They knew well and loved the 'Stories of the Bible,' and they learned the sweet and simple poems of the Victorian era. Their toys were few so they played with horses and dogs, calves and rabbits and chickens. Their radius was limited to the few miles that could be covered by riding and driving."

"Miss Charlotte," as her mother called her, even before her teens, was first schooled by pre-ministerial student, Robert Nelson, at Burrland, from 1891-1895. Next year, a move to Baltimore in the winter was decided upon: "A Northern atmosphere would be best and also, the Tabbs and Harrisons were there." There, home was 1409 Linden Avenue, "a respectable but not especially stylish neighborhood, but the house was a gem."

Miss Charlotte went to school for the first time in 1898, age 15, at the Misses Middleton's School: "Several sweet old ladies had started private schools and made me the most flattering reductions. They were making valiant efforts to support themselves–Southerners who had come north after the war." Each of the three Noland girls went to a different private school. The four boys attended the same public school. Bored with the Misses Middletons, Charlotte asked her father one snowy day if she could skip school to go sledding. "Fine," said Cuthbert, but next day, daughter forgot to bring the excuse note he had written. Her teacher had seen her sledding, did not believe her excuse, and that closed her days at the Misses Middleton–the first of several schools from which Charlotte never graduated.

Summers were spent at Burrland, where in 1898 she and sister Rosalie, prompted by a cultural lack among the males, withdrew to poetry and prose by starting a literary club. The works were written in five-cent notebooks purchased by each girl. On the first page of Charlotte's is the heading: "Short Stories and Poems by the Members of the Literary Club of Loudoun County, Virginia, Summer 1898."

And below is the scribbling of one of her brothers: "This book is full of Hot-Air," followed by his words, "Hot Air," written on every page. The girls generally escaped such tactics by meeting in the hayloft of the Burrland barn.

The six members signed different names to their works. Charlotte signed hers "W. Shakespere," because she had a beau named William. Sister Rosalie signed hers "Tomas Moore," because her suitor was a farmer's son named Tommy. Nellie Tabb became John Milton—her swain was John. Eleanor Perrin was Walter Scott, probably for the same reason, and two unknown lasses were Charles Dickens and Robert Browning, with one poem signed "Robert Browning to Elizabeth Browning."

One of Shakespere's ventures won the bard $25, first prize in the Ivory Soap contest in *Saint Nicholas Magazine*. With apologies to *Macbeth*, its last four lines ran, " 'It's Duncan's blood,' the man replied. She tries the fearful stains to hide. 'Why don't she wash 'em, I'll be gosh, with Ivory Soap?' said Uncle Josh." Charlotte spent the prize money to pay for an operation to correct the hair lip of the family housekeeper's daughter, playmate Keziah Thomas.

PHOTO COURTESY FOXCROFT SCHOOL

The porch at Burrland (destroyed in 1962)

Charlotte's first job was teaching athletics to the girls at St. Timothy's, Catonsville, Maryland, a school begun by Polly and Sally Carter of Albemarle County about 1870. A hint of patronage was there, as Cuthbert's sister, Bessie, married Robert Carter, Polly's and Sally's brother. But as the school was without a gym, Charlotte left shortly. She found her gym at the Baltimore YWCA, and promptly hired it out, interesting "quite a number of lazy socialites, who had made their debuts and had time hanging heavy…" Charlotte worked them on high and broad jumps, running, and basketball.

Charlotte then applied to teach at the select Bryn Mawr School in Baltimore. The headmistress was the famous Greek and classics scholar,

Edith Hamilton, who rarely ventured to take a look at the gym. Applying for a job, Charlotte convinced Edith to let her see the gym, and there, on the floor was the male Swedish gym teacher groaning from a wrenched back. Miss Edith turned to Miss Charlotte, saying, "What can I do?" Charlotte suggested herself. Miss Hamilton agreed and promptly went back to her Greek.

Studying at Oxford University, England, in 1904, Charlotte rented a horse on Saturday afternoon, her usual custom, and soon came upon a beautiful entranceway, framed by a rose arbor. The estate was owned by a Major Foxcroft. As Miss Charlotte recounted, on tape, in 1968, "The name hit me right! I took it back and kept it, and as soon as I bought Locust Lawn, I named it Foxcroft."

Geographically it hit too, for in 1905, Harry Worcester Smith, appropriately from Worcester, Massachusetts, heralded the return of the foxhunt to Loudoun and Fauquier with his staging of a British-American Foxhound match at nearby Upperville. The hunt country had arrived. Croft, an Old English word for a piece of ground (under seven acres), close to the house and used for tillage and pasture, by Miss Charlotte's time had become synonymous for the best land on a farm.

"One early afternoon in 1905, up drove Virginia's Senator-to-be-Harry Byrd, with sister Rosie, and a good-looking horse and runabout. As we sat on the porch, our newly installed telephone rang. A telegram from Mrs. Randall in Baltimore–Katherine was sick and could not come to us. What hard luck!

" 'What can we do about the party?' lamented Rosie. 'No guest of honor.'

"Charlotte looked speculatively at Harry, his round pink cheeks and curly golden hair, then said, 'Harry, you will have to be Katherine tonight.'

"So at eight o'clock we sat out on the porch with our lovely house guest, waiting for the friends to arrive.

" 'Katherine' had on a lovely picture hat, her curls almost hidden by the floppy brim. She wore a sweet-flowered lawn dress, open only slightly at the neck, and a scarf was around her (rather stout) waist, and a long full skirt.

" 'Now remember, Harry,' came Charlotte's last directive, 'you must not cross your knees, and you must keep your skirt over your shoes.'

Harry lifted his skirt, showing large manly shoes, and promised to do his best.

"Rosie spoke up, 'It's a pretty dirty trick, Harry, that Charlotte is playing on you, but you do look awful pretty.'

"As the relatives and friends came along, they were introduced to 'Miss Randall' who stood up and bowed formally and dropped back to her seat. Then came Louise Haxall, who had told us she was distantly related to Katherine. She hopped out of her buggy and skipped up to the two porch steps, and as 'Katherine' stood up, Louise held out her arms. 'Oh, I'm so glad to know you at last, for we are really kissing cousins, aren't we?'

"The fair lady returned Louise's kiss heartily and sat down with a giggle. We all gathered around and conversation was general, and Harry got so interested he forgot to be careful and hitched up his skirt! There were those big feet in plain view, and before any of us could hide them, Louise saw! She exclaimed: 'What is this; who are you?' And Harry rose up trying to apologize, and Charlotte broke in with a laugh, and everyone began to laugh and fire questions, but poor Louise was really upset: 'You had no right to kiss me, you fooled me and it's horrid of all of you.' I thought she'd weep. 'I do apologize,' said Harry boldly, taking off his ladylike hat, 'but I certainly did enjoy that kiss, and mayn't I call you Cousin?' "

Before Foxcroft there were the 1910-1913 summers at Burrland, where Miss Charlotte ran her "Farmerettes," a camp for some 20 to 30 youngsters. One of her youngest was cousin Stuart Symington (later Missouri's senator) then five years old. One night of intense thunder and lightning, he ran from his tent and up to Miss Charlotte's room, where he was found at the foot of her bed when she awoke.

Wallis Warfield Simpson, later Duchess of Windsor, was a Burrland Farmerette at ages 15 and 16 in 1910-1911. There she met her first beau, Lloyd Tabb, a 17-year-old who lived at Glen Ora, some 50 years later the retreat of President and Mrs. John F. Kennedy. Wallis and the other girls would often spend Sundays at Glen Ora, for there was a tennis court and Sunday supper. A horse by the name of Almo Dobbin Spec Creature pulled the wagon the one mile from Burrland to Glen Ora. In the wagon the girls sang: "Almo, sweet Almo, where have you been? What is your home, dear? What is your phone, dear? Your number, please give. A wedding ring is the only ring Almo can wear."

Miss Charlotte decided that she wanted to start a school for girls in the spring of 1913, and that summer she herded her Farmerettes to Locust Lawn, home of George Inniss Hartley. Convinced that this was the place, she borrowed $5,000 from Peoples Bank in Leesburg–one of her many beaus was an officer–to build "The Porch House," on property that was only rented.

On June 28, 1914, Serbian nationalists assassinated Archduke Franz Ferdinand, heir apparent to the throne of Austria-Hungary. On August 1, Germany declared war on Russia. Travel to Europe was curtailed. The girls who would have gone to school in Switzerland had nothing to do. They were still too young to make their debuts. In short–an auspicious time for the debut that fall of Foxcroft School.

Tales of Miss Charlotte's Baltimore gym classes and Burrland Farmerettes spread–her students were always her best advertisers–and her discreet catalogue titled, "Foxcroft School For Girls at the Foxcroft Farm in the Piedmont Valley, Loudoun County, Virginia, Out-of-Door Life and Study," made its way into prominent Virginia and Northeastern homes. Parents read:

> Foxcroft marks a new era in the management of girls' schools, since it is the first to combine genuine country life with school life. The increasing tendency in America toward leading a country life has particularly manifested itself in the neighborhood in which Foxcroft is situated, hence its selection for the carrying out of the School's plans. Foxcroft aims to cultivate to the highest degree the physique of its pupils by means of the delightful sports and pastimes of the present day.
>
> The best of the present with the best of the past. Lessons and pleasures are guided by wise and judicious gentle women whose aim is the preserving, the training, and the recounting of tradition to revive in its pupils the refined manners, cultivated minds and sympathetic personalities which have made the women of the South world-famous.

Courses of study covered five years of Latin, covering Caesar, Cicero, and Virgil; five years of French; four of German; and four of drawing. "Mens Sana in Corpore Sano"–A Healthy Mind and A Healthy Body– was Charlotte's and Foxcroft's motto.

One thousand dollars covered board, tuition, and riding expenses. "The outside expenses are one hundred dollars a year for music lessons, five dollars a year for church sitting [at Middleburg's Emmanuel], fifty dollars a year for laundry and mending, two dollars per trip for pupil and trunk between school and station [at The Plains]. Pupils' own horses can be boarded at the School stables for twenty-five dollars a month, which includes shoeing."

Reasonable rates when compared to the steamer voyage and stay in Switzerland, though about three times the cost of the two nearby girls' schools: The Fauquier Female Institute, a mainstay since 1857, where Nellie Butler was "a born teacher"; and the Warrenton Country School For Girls of Madame Lea M. Bouligny, started in 1914. John D. Chapin's Loudoun Select School For Young Ladies at Bluemont, begun 1910, closed the year before Foxcroft opened.

The Brick House at Foxcroft, built by William Benton PHOTO COURTESY FOSCROFT SCHOOOL

That day was September 25, 1914. "God bless her," her mother prayed, "and let her succeed with this school of her dreams." That morning, her mother recalled, "such excitement in the Washington Station! Miss Rosie was to be recognized by a white boutonniere; the girls were to wear a red label or flower." They took the Manassas Gap branch of the Southern Railway to The Plains, then by wagon on the Halfway toll road (five cents a wheel), 12 miles to school, beholding a landscape depicted in the school catalogue: "In this happy valley the inhabitants manage their own estates and farms, and for their diversion hunt foxes, and rabbits, shoot, fish, and ride."

Miss Charlotte wrote in the first Foxcroft yearbook, the 1915 *Tally Ho!*, "For years a school of this kind has been my pet idea, but it was with many fears and misgivings that I started it this fall, and no one can ever imagine the great load that rested on my heart the night 24 perfectly strange girls appeared at my door."

Girls only? Not quite; there was Francis Green, cousin of Edith Kennedy Sands, neighbor and friend of Miss Charlotte. He was the only boy ever to attend Foxcroft–though he did not board–being among the six day scholars. His headmistress related that "at the age of 15 he showed great composure in this unusual situation."

After a bit of orientation and study, school started in earnest in October–no self respecting woman ever worked before October. Miss Charlotte "decided on a coon-hunt for all who did not weep from homesickness! So on the early evening of October 3, they followed two huntsmen and two coon dogs, who soon treed their prey. But upon felling the tree, it smashed into a smaller one, and the coon scampered away. 'The coons generally do get away,' pronounced our authority, Miss Charlotte."

Before Christmas recess, "one girl burst out crying. 'I don't really want to go home!' And after the recess, a visitor stopped by the Porch House and asked Miss Rosie: 'How much did this building cost?' Taken aback, but quick mentally, she doubled the sum. 'About $10,000, I believe.' " A few weeks later, a letter from a big foundation came "stating that she had heard of this school, where a girl wept at having to leave it for a holiday, so it must be a rather unusual type and it was her pleasure to send this check."

Charlotte was able to make a little extra money by allowing everyone to hold it–for a charge of five cents. "Who has ever seen, much less held, a $10,000 check?"

On March 31, 1915, Miss Charlotte bought her school, "A tract of land known as "Foxcroft" or the "Rogers' farm" containing 182 acres situated near the Pot House," and 82 acres of the Furr Farm. The selling price was $21,000—$300 from Miss Charlotte, the remainder from Edith Sands and the generosity of her husband, a New York Quaker, Daniel C. Sands. "You'll pay it back to me sometime," Edith said. On March 9, 1918, Miss Charlotte gained full possession of the school by paying off her debt.

Later she purchased additional buildings (cost $15,000) from Major Hartley, ready to go off to World War I. Two days before the major set sail, for the third time she approached her beau at Peoples Bank, got her third loan, and finally paid off her first note. A Virginia adage states character is the only thing on which one can safely loan money. Taking the night train to New York, she concluded the deal at the old Hotel Belmont, two hours before Hartley sailed. Miss Charlotte promised him that if he ever had a daughter, she would be educated at Foxcroft. Major Hartley complied, and Barbara Hartley was graduated, Class of '41.

Keziah Thomas, a black woman and Miss Charlotte's companion since 1890, by now was her right hand. Charlotte always sought her advice. What do the girls need? What should they do and what shouldn't they do?–such as no more coed campus dances after spring of 1921, when some young gentlemen refused to go home at 4 a.m. and were found at dawn, sleeping under the boxwood.

Well into the '30s, Miss Charlotte would come into a class and tell the students to "close that book and come out and get onto your horse."

A class 'disruption'–Note Miss Charlotte on sidesaddle

Photo courtesy Foxcroft School

Her sister, Rosie, then teaching English, told her she was very disruptive. Miss Charlotte agreed and proceeded to fire her sister, who left for the academic pastures of St. Catherine's, Richmond, where she became headmistress.

Christina Wayman, a Scotswoman from Dundee, was largely responsible for turning an atmosphere somewhat country-clubbish to an atmosphere somewhat academic in the early '20s. After the slight depressions following the Great War, parents began hinting at college and jobs after graduation. And while Miss Charlotte never emphasized the academic side–it was becoming too in vogue–she at least gave it equal time. She always countered educational trends. If all the schools were doing it, she didn't. During the Depression, when everyone lowered tuitions, Foxcroft raised theirs $500–and had a longer waiting list. She was stubborn, but she had a talent for making a person out of a nonentity. She could read human nature, and had intuition, if no formal education, which she readily admitted, and relished–especially in academic circles. Once when attending an educational luncheon in New York City, everyone had name plates with Ph.D, L.H.D., and the like after his name. Charlotte had a set of initials too–M.F.H. for Master of Foxhounds.

On June 3, 1958 she received another set of initials, the L.H.D. (Doctor of Humane Letters) from Columbia University, presented by President Grayson Kirk. The citation read, in part: "Intellectual excellence, moral discipline, service to community, and faith are the Foxcroft credo–lived most of all, as example, by Charlotte Haxall Noland."

Equally telling were words read by new Foxcroft headmaster Van-Santvoord Merle-Smith Jr., at a memorial service at St. James' Episcopal Church, New York City, October 29, 1969. They were taken from a letter written by Miss Charlotte to her alumnae in 1919: "Keep up with the times, don't be narrow, have few rules, good hard work and much fun, pile up traditions and remember 'with God all things are possible.' "

PHOTO COURTESY FOXCROFT SCHOOL

Charlotte Noland's legacy, Foxcroft School, ca. 1970

Acknowledgment

Our thanks to the following persons for their time, effort and for their special memories. Without their generosity, the preservation of these recollections would not have been possible.

William Altizer, Neville Lemmon Atkinson, Ada Gibson Auty,
Elizabeth Ayres, Nancy Chappelear Baird, Charles W. Ball,
Isabelle Baltimore, Erskine Bedford, John Perry Bodmer, Joyce Bowie,
Jimand Frances Bowman, Ruth Brittlebank, Philip Hopkins Broun,
George White Brown, Louis W. Carter Jr., Rosa Carter,
B. Curtis Chappelear., Terry Gaskins Colbert, Neal Corum,
Nancy Cook Cotten, Anne Slater Coyner, Mrs. Charles Davis,
Mary Custis Lee deButts, Philip Deely, John Divine, Emily de Zerega,
James E. Douglass, James E. Douglass Jr., Erman Downs,
Dr. Ann C. Fred, Dr. Edwin Broun Fred, Carl Furr, Richard H. Gaskins Jr.,
Anne Gochnauer, Richard Gookin, John K. Gott,
Mildred Boyde Gray, Eva Kines Hall, Lizzie Stewart Harris, Janet Harrison,
Ann Stewart Hatcher, Helen Helmick, Etta Furr Hensley, J. Terry Hirst,
Kiku Hoagland, Mr. and Mrs Thomas E. Hoff, Bishop Howard,
Bishop Howard Jr.., Mrs. Robert Humphrey, Robert L. Humphrey Jr.,
Fritz Hutchison, Jack Hutchison, Louisa Hutchison, Thomas B. Hutchison,
Lelia Bentley Jackson, Mary F. Jackson, Lucy Keith, Welby Kenny,
Richard and Dixie Lee Lodge Lake, Elizabeth H. Lemmon,
Evalyn Adams Litton, Monte Lloyd, S. Preston Luck Jr..,
Mrs. Thomas Lynch, the Reverend Walter F. Malloy,
Mr. and Mrs. James P. McCormick, Loyal McMillin, Myrtle McQuay,
Karlton L. Monroe, Mr. and Mrs. Glanwood Moore, George Morison,
Sallie Harris Morison, James Napper, Don Nunes, Mildred Parham,
Murrel Lee Partlow, Franklin W. Payne, Mary C. Peacock, Ann Perricone,
Mary Howard Peterson, John S. Pettibone, Rosamond Pettibone,

Wallace W. Phillips, Cora L. Poles, Mrs. John T. Ramey, Mrs. A. C. Randolph, Theodora Ayer Randolph, Mary K. Reamer, Alberta Reed, Morris and Thelma Rector, Emma and Gracie Reid, Charles Franklin Riticor, John Thomas Riticor, Peggy Roberts, Edward Rose,Charles Sacra, Ruth Basil Scott, Katherine Slater, Annie Smith, Bernice Smith, Mr. and Mrs.Curtis Smith, Janice Smith, Mollie Buchanan Smith, Nathan Smith, Thelma Smith, R. F. S. Starr, the Reverend Melvin Steadman, Ethel Smith Stewart, Geneva Bowman Stewart, the Reverend and Mrs. H. James M. Stewart, Mr. and Mrs. James Stewart Jr., Janet Tayloe, C. B. Tavenner, the Reverend Eugene E. Terry, Allin Tibbs, William E. Trout, Charles H. Turner, James F. Tyler, John Marvin Tyler, T. Francis Tyler, Melvin A. Warren, the Reverend Wadell Waters, Mr. and Mrs. Leopold Weidlein, Esdelia Willis, Tucker Withers, E. B. White, Annie Mae Whitney, Richard Wiltshire, and Christine Wright.

Bibliography

The History of Middleburg and Vicinity provides comprehensive coverage of the area covered by zip code 20117. It does not venture east of Dover or west of Atoka. Its detailed bibliography is worth consulting for works not mentioned here. I wrote the book for the Middleburg Bicentennial Committee in 1987.

Of other works concerning the town, there are three walking tours and one combined walk and a drive. The most detailed, though a bit dry, is *Destination Middleburg: A Walking Tour Into the Past*, by architectural historians Maral S. Kalbian and Leila O. W. Boyer. Middleburg Beautification and Preservation published the work 2001.

That same year resident Audrey Windsor Bergner published her *Visitors Guide to Middleburg, Virginia and the Surrounding John Singleton Mosby Heritage Area.*

Other vignettes appear in long-time resident Loyal McMillan's "A Walk with History," privately printed in 1987, and my walk-through in the 1975 *Guide to Loudoun*, which also features a Route 50 driving tour and other driving tours covering the domain of *Loudoun Discovered*'s Volume Three.

The title tells about all, except that there are some fine photos, in Mrs. Bergner's *Old Plantations and Historic Homes Around Middleburg, Virginia: and the Families Who Lived and Loved Within Their Walls.* New York: Cornwall Books, 2001.

In a more chatty vein, we have Vicky Moon's *The Middleburg Mystique: A Peek Inside the Gates*...Capital Books in Sterling published the work in 2001—a big year for female authors.

For an earlier quasi-history see Vme Edom Smith's *Middleburg and Nearby.* Middleburg: Robert and Gwen Dobson, 1986. The "Nearby" extends from Aldie to Upperville.

Numerous other pre-1987 works in the "Mystique" category are cited in *The History of Middleburg* bibliography.

A church history worth mentioning because it provides context, is *Emmanuel Episcopal Church: Johns Parish*, by parishioner Chester Low, 1993.

Of the other towns, Upperville and Paris, from their beginnings through early 19th century are covered well in B. Curtis Chappelear's posthumously published *Maps and Notes Pertaining to The Upper Section of Fauquier County*. Warrenton: Fauquier Antiquarian Society, 1954. Be sure you get an edition with the foldout map in it. The predecessor of the Upperville resume appeared in the Marshall newspaper, *The Chief Justice*, June 4, 1929.

Of more recent vintage, a valuable reference tool is the bound "Historic Survey: Upperville, Va.,"—unusual because each building is drawn rather than photographed. It's undated (ca. 1975), and my copy bears no author's or artist's name.

Upperville is also the subject of Kitty Slater's well-written piece in *SPUR of Virginia*, Winter 1971.

Vignettes of town appear in *Amy's Family: Descendants of Casper Rinker* by Marcia Y. Supplee. Stephen's City: Commercial Press, 1995.

Walking tours of Upperville and Paris appear in my 1976 *The Guide to Fauquier*, which also features a driving tour along Route 50, west from Atoka.

Drawing from the above sources, which he fully cites, is Kevin Mettinger's resume of Upperville in *The Fauquier Citizen*, July 20, 1990.

Paris's problems with the modern age are noted in Paul Hodges's *The Washington Post* article, E1, Jan. 16, 1993.

Had I redone the *Loudoun Times-Mirror* series I would have included the hamlet known to most as Palmer's Mill. Some of its history, though, appears in my *Washington Post* article in the "Loudoun Extra" section, Jan. 21, 2001.

Standing alone in its class is Kitty Slater's *The Hunt Country of America*, which first came out in 1967 (South Brunswick, N. J.: A. S. Barnes). A "revised" edition dates from 1973, a "revisited" edition from 1987, and a final edition, subtitled *Then and Now*, from 1997. Upperville's Virginia Reel published the last edition. The books' fine photos have changed from edition to edition—a quartet of who's who on horseback.

Foxhunting history also has its magnum opus, Alexander Mackey-Smith's *The American Foxhound 1747-1976*. Millwood, Va.: The American Foxhound Club, 1968. In 1987 I wrote that 100 leather-bound copies sold for $45; 1,000 cloth-bound copies for $25.

Civil War history centers on the June 17-21, 1863, turnpike battles prior to Gettysburg. The finest account is Robert F. O'Neill's *The Cavalry Battles of Aldie, Middleburg and Upperville*...Lynchburg: H. E. Howard, 1993. His excellent cassette tape, "Prelude to Gettysburg," issued by the John Singleton Mosby Heritage Area in 1997, also covers what O'Neill terms "small but important riots."

Not quite as detailed is Wilbur Sturtevant Nye's *Here Comes The Rebels*. Louisiana State Press, 1965.

Among numerous other accounts: Roy P. Stonesifer Jr., "The Union Cavalry Comes of Age," in *Battles Lost and Won: Essays from Civil War History*, ed. John T. Hubbell. Westport, Conn.: Greenwood Press, 1975: Marshall D. Krolick, "Lee vs. Stuart: The Gettysburg Altercation," in *Virginia Country* (February, 1984) and my *Civil War in Fauquier*..., Warrenton: The Fauquier Bank, 1985. That work also covers other area Civil War incidents, as does the aforementioned *History of Middleburg.*

Nearly a score of books pertain to the campaigns and life of partisan ranger John Singleton Mosby: The final five, in order of publication: Kevin H. Siepel, *Rebel: The Life and Times of John Singleton Mosby.* New York: St. Martin's Press, 1983; Jeffrey D. Wert, *Mosby's Rangers.* New York: Simon and Schuster, 1990; Thomas J. Evans and James M. Moyer, *Mosby's Confederacy: A Guide to the Roads and Sites of Colonel John Singleton Mosby*. Shippensburg, Pa.: White Mane, 1991; Hugh C. Keen and Horace Mewborn, *43rd Battalion Virginia Cavalry: Mosby's Command.* Lynchburg: H. E. Howard, 1993; James A Ramage, *Gray Ghost: The Life of Col. John Singleton Mosby*. University Press of Kentucky, 1999.

Of these works, Siepel's is a complete biography; the others concentrate on Mosby's wartime exploits. Keen and Mewborn have a superlative roster but no index. Wert has stronger writing and photographs. Evans and Moyer organize their book into tours and present fine photos and appendices. Wert calls the Ramage book the best biography of Mosby.

Horace Mewborn's scholarship is evident in his cassette tape, "Historical Events of the 43rd Battalion...From Truro Church, Fairfax, to Atoka...," 1999. The cassette fails to mention the author, citing only the narrator, Robert O'Neill. Mewborn's "In the Wake of Antietam," is scheduled for release this autumn. The John Singleton Mosby Heritage area has sponsored both cassette tapes.

Regarding biographies of area notables, Charles Fenton Mercer received an early plaudit in kin James Mercer Garnett's *Biographical Sketch*...Richmond: Whittet & Shepperson, 1911.

More accessible works about Mercer: Douglas R. Egerton's *Charles Fenton Mercer and the Trial of National Conservatism*. Jackson: University Press of Mississippi, 1989; the article centering on education by Robert Allen Carter in the 1997 *Bulletin of the Historical Society of Loudoun County*. The article is drawn from Carter's 1988 Ph.D. dissertation, "Virginia Federalist in dissent..."

"A brief account of Miss Charlotte's life and times as recounted by her family and by her alumnae" is the subtitle of the nostalgic *Charlotte Haxall Noland 1883-1969*, edited by Mary Custis Lee deButts and Rosalie Noland Woodland. Foxcroft School issued the book in 1971.

And since Thomas, sixth Lord Fairfax often rode down the old Belhaven Road—as well as being the grantor for nearly all land in Loudoun—I cite Stuart E. Brown's *Virginia Baron: The Story of Thomas, 6th Lord Fairfax*. Berryville: Chesapeake Book Co., 1965.

Much about his life and land grants is included in Fairfax Harrison's rare *Virginia Land Grants*, privately printed for the author in 1925.

"Civil War Diary of Ida Powell Dulany," is all the information we have regrarding a printed and bound edition, the title set against a background of my map of Fauquier County. Some of the lady from Oakley's dairies–along with the pithy diaries, letters, and other jottings of her family members–appear in *The Dulanys of Welbourne: A Family in Mosby's Confederacy*. Margaret Ann Vogtsberger edited and annotated the work in passable fashion. Berryville: Rockbridge Publishing,1995.

While on the subject of Civil War-era diaries, those of Middleburg's Catherine Broun and Mary Cochran, deserve publishing with good commentary. Several excerpts appear in *The History of Middleburg*.

Paul Mellon's autobiography, *Reflections In a Silver Spoon: A Memoir* presents insights into why his family foundations donated funds for so many worthwhile projects in Loudoun and upper Fauquier. New York's W. Morrow published the book in 1992.

Nancy Gartrell Lee receives an overdue tribute in the *Fauquier* magazine, 8, 1 (Spring 1995). Louisa Woodville wrote the profile.

In the miscellaneous category, my "LE" article in the *Post*, Nov. 5, 2000, deals with the history and surveys of the Loudoun-Fauquier line.

The same section of the *Post*, Susan Saulny's coverage of the fall beagling trials at The Institute has a lot of information, Nov. 8, 1998.

A planning document of note for the far southwest of Loudoun is the 1999 "Beaverdam Creek Historic Roadways District Study," which I prepared for the Goose Creek Association.

Regarding other works of countywide interest, the best and only one worth its salt is Charles Preston Poland Jr.'s *From Frontier to Suburbia*, published in 1979 at Marceline, Missouri, by Walsworth Publishing.

Full of exquisite detail, though only for the county's first decade, is John Phillips II's *The Historian's Guide to Loudoun County*, volume 1, issued by Phillips's Goose Creek Productions in 1996.

For a short read, try my chronological "1,000 Years of Loudoun," issued by *The Washington Post* in 2000. This compendium initially appeared in each December 1999 "Loudoun Extra" edition of the *Post.*

Fairfax Harrison's 1924 classic, *Landmarks of Old Prince William*, reprinted at least twice, covers a myriad of subjects from the American Indian era of the 17th century through to the early 1800s. Mr. Harrison's aristocratic prose may delight, but the book's organization can baffle. Footnotes are lengthy and erudite.

Two venerable books are yet valuable for certain tidbits. James W. Head, a Leesburger, was the first person to try his hand at writing a county history. *The History and Comprehensive Description of Loudoun County*...was published by his hometown Park View Press in 1908. Thirty years later, Leesburg lawyer Harrison Williams tried his hand at *Legends of Loudoun*, Richmond: Garrett and Massie, 1938. The title gives you a warning as to some of his deft prose's accuracy.

Two detailed *Loudoun Times-Mirror* series, the first on the history of planning and zoning in Loudoun, the second on the Great Depression, appear respectively in the Oct. 9, 15, 23, and 30, 1986, issues; and the Feb. 18, 25; Mar. 4, 11, 18, 1982 issues.

Other countywide works relevant to this book are fully cited in the Volume Two bibliography on pages 140ff.

Relevant area maps: My *John Singleton Mosby Heritage Area* map, published by the Heritage Area in 1996. Scale: One inch equals eight-tenths of a mile. Also see my *Snickersville Turnpike: Virginia*, a bird's-eye view in full color, published by the Turnpike Association in 1997. Its companion, ...*Snickersville Turnpike: Delineating the Land Grants*, scale: one inch equals two-thirds of a mile, shows original land-grant boundaries and owners within a few miles of the pike.

Showing land-grant boundaries and owners for entire western Loudoun are the three maps diligently and masterfully prepared by Netti Yantis-Schreiner in 1997-98. Boundaries are plotted on the U. S. Geological Survey's 1:24,000 maps. Sheets C and D cover the area of Volume Three.

For the horsey and foxhunting set, Margot L. Skinner's 1919 *"TRI" Hunting Map* initiated this genre. Scale: one inch equals one and three-quarters of a mile (approx.).

Following in her stead, Colonel Harold E. Potter of Aldie used Army Map Service quadrangles to locate hunting fixtures in his circa 1955 *Guide Map for Piedmont – Middleburg and Orange County Hunts.* Scale: 1:48,000.

Others of this type are: *The Virginia Hunt Country*, showing boundaries of all hunts from Orange and Madison Counties north to the Potomac. Scale: one inch equals 4.2 miles (approx.), and *Fixtures: Orange County and Middleburg Hunts and Piedmont Foxhounds.* Scale: one inch equals nine-tenths of a mile (approx.). I drew the former map in 1978, the latter in 1981.

Also see my Tri-Counties Map of *Upper Prince William, Lower Loudoun, and East Fauquier*, covering the Middleburg area and its eastern environs. Scale: one inch equals seven-eighths of a mile (approx.), 1994.

In the rare category is the ca. 1780 map in pieces featuring the Carolina Road, fully cited in the Volume Two bibliography. The 1801 Jonathan Lovett map, *Distances Leesburg/Winchester Virginia*, scale: one inch equals 1,000 poles, depicts today's Routes 7, and 50, and the connecting Snickersville Turnpike. *A Map of the Paved Road from the Little River Bridge at Aldie to the Shenandoah*—today's Snickersville Turnpike—is dated 1820 by someone who was not the anonymous map-maker. The map is not to scale.

Town plats of more than passing interest are three Middleburg plats: the first dates from the early 19th century, map-maker unknown; the second, *Plot of Middleburg*, 1883, by Jonah Tavenner; the third, *Tax Plat of Middleburg, Va.* by Trundle and [Thomas] Fendall, August 1933. Scale: one inch equals 400 feet. The last map appears in full on the end cover of *The History of Middleburg.*

George Love's ca. 1810 plat of Paris and 1828 plat of Upperville appear in the Chappelear book, previously cited. Love's 1826 survey of the Loudoun-Fauquier line is also special because it locates houses and names residents.

Overall county maps of note: First, the 1853 effort of Yardley Taylor, titled *Map of Loudoun County, Virginia, from Actual Surveys.* Published in color by Thomas Reynolds and Robert Pearsall Smith of Philadelphia, the map's scale is 1 inch equals one and three-eighths miles (approx.). The Janney brothers, natives of Mr. Taylor's Lincoln, reprinted the map at a scale of 1 inch equals 1 mile. The U. S. Topographical Engineers' 1862 [Map of] *North-Eastern Virginia and Vicinity of Washington* draws heavily from Yardley Taylor's map.

The U. S. Post Office Department's circa 1915 *Rural Delivery Routes, Loudoun County, Virginia* is the next detailed map of the entire county to follow that of Mr. Taylor. Its scale, 1 inch equals 1 mile. Piggybacking on that map, at the same scale, but in color, is Oscar L. Emerick's 1923 map showing public schools, simply titled *Loudoun County, Virginia.*

U. S. Coast and Geodetic Survey, Geological Survey, and Army Map Service 1:125,000, 1:62,500, and 1:24,000 maps of the 1880s through 1960s show the then-slow patterns of growth. As an adjunct, the 1937 and 1950 aerial photographs, 1 inch equals 1,320 feet, flown by the Soil and Conservation Service, are valuable in regard to where structures once stood and where old roads cut through the landscape. The clarity of the 1937 photos remains unexcelled.

Virginia's highway department, now VDOT, has issued county road maps since 1932, with that year's map naming the roads as well as giving numbers that were changed in 1936. Editions of the 1940s and '50s also show rural and village buildings, often in a less-than-accurate manner. The maps' scale: 1 inch equals 2 miles.

Index

A complete index of the people, organizations, buildings, roads, events, and other matters included in *Loudoun Discovered* would contain well over 10,000 entries. To facilitate searching for this information, two approaches have been taken.

First, each volume includes a summary index, such as that which follows, of the information which features most prominently in the volume.

Second, a full text search capability covering all five volumes of *Loudoun Discovered* can be accessed through the website of the Friends of the Thomas Balch Library. See www.balchfriends.org.